Also by Peter Cole

POETRY

Rift ▪ *Hymns & Qualms* ▪ *What Is Doubled: Poems 1981–1998* ▪ *Things on Which I've Stumbled* ▪ *The Invention of Influence*

TRANSLATION

Selected Poems of Shmuel HaNagid ▪ *Selected Poems of Solomon Ibn Gabirol* ▪ *Love & Selected Poems*, by Aharon Shabtai ▪ *From Island to Island*, by Harold Schimmel ▪ *Qasida*, by Harold Schimmel ▪ *Never Mind: Twenty Poems and a Story*, by Taha Muhammad Ali (with Yahya Hijazi and Gabriel Levin) ▪ *So What: New & Selected Poems, 1971–2005*, by Taha Muhammad Ali (with Yahya Hijazi and Gabriel Levin) ▪ *Collected Poems*, by Avraham Ben Yitzhak ▪ *The Heart Is Katmandu*, by Yoel Hoffmann ▪ *The Shunra and the Schmetterling*, by Yoel Hoffmann ▪ *Curriculum Vitae*, by Yoel Hoffmann ▪ *Moods*, by Yoel Hoffmann ▪ *J'Accuse*, by Aharon Shabtai ▪ *War & Love, Love & War: New and Selected Poems*, by Aharon Shabtai ▪ *The Dream of the Poem: Hebrew Poetry from Muslim and Christian Spain, 950–1492* ▪ *The Poetry of Kabbalah: Mystical Verse from the Jewish Tradition*

OTHER

Hebrew Writers on Writing (editor) ▪ *Sacred Trash: The Lost and Found World of the Cairo Geniza* (with Adina Hoffman)

HYMNS & QUALMS

PETER COLE

New and Selected

Farrar, Straus and Giroux / New York

HYMNS
QUALMS

Poems and Translations

Farrar, Straus and Giroux
175 Varick Street, New York 10014

The Library of Congress has cataloged the hardcover edition as follows:
Names: Cole, Peter, 1957– author.
Title: Hymns & qualms : new and selected poems and translations / Peter Cole.
Other titles: Hymns and qualms
Description: First edition. | New York, NY : Farrar, Straus and Giroux, 2017.
Identifiers: LCCN 2016041329 | ISBN 9780374173883 (hardback)
Subjects: BISAC: POETRY / American / General.
Classification: LCC PS3553.O47325 A6 2017 | DDC 811/.54—dc23
LC record available at https://lccn.loc.gov/2016041329

Paperback ISBN: 978-0-374-53770-8

Our books may be purchased in bulk for promotional, educational, or
business use. Please contact your local bookseller or the Macmillan Corporate
and Premium Sales Department at 1-800-221-7945, extension 5442, or by
e-mail at MacmillanSpecialMarkets@macmillan.com.

www.fsgbooks.com
www.twitter.com/fsgbooks
www.facebook.com/fsgbooks

P1

Unless otherwise indicated, translations are from the Hebrew.

For A—

     as (in) Always

          between these lines

CONTENTS

AUTHOR'S NOTE

For almost as long as I've written poems, I've translated them. Over time, the two modes in me came to feel like one, or at least like aspects of a single impulse. Maybe because they always were. In 1981, when I first went to Jerusalem, I was, a little strangely, looking for a Hebrew that would give me English. Small surprise that I found it "slant," in the Jewish poems of medieval Spain (which emerged through Arabic) and with the living, language-shifting poets of the old-new city where I still pay rent; that this brought me to Galilean kabbalah and the mysteries of reception, which is part of what kabbalah can mean; and that the Palestinian poetry of those hills would eventually follow. In between came just about everything—life.

This book enfolds a movement between these various modes and worlds and into the vital transfer that translation is—from sensation to expression, from one person's language and age to another's. In primary ways, as on these pages, "original" poems and "translations" intertwine: hence the double helix of this whole. The earliest pieces here took shape mostly but not only in Jerusalem; the more recent found their curious and often circuitous paths to paper on desks and park benches in New Haven, along the coasts of Cycladic islands, and again in Jerusalem, albeit a very different city from the one where the writing began. Throughout, there were friends and goads, trials, wonders, misgivings, weathers, trees, catastrophes, and pleasures. I've tried to honor them all.

P.C.

New Poems, New Translations

EVERY SINGLE PERSON

Every single person you meet,
Philo wrote, it's said—Everyone—
is fighting a very great battle.
Except that no one is able to find
where he said it, or what he thought
the burden might be that brings it on.
Still, it's almost certainly true—
and so he added, perhaps, be kind.

THROUGH THE SLAUGHTER

and Bialik

Sky—have mercy.
When flechettes fly
    forth from a shell,
    shot by a tank
        taking Ezekiel's
        chariot's name—

When their thin fins
invisibly whiz,
    whiffling the air
    like angels' wings—
        their metal feathers
        guiding them in—

When their hooks rip
through random flesh
    in a promise of land
    with its boring sun—
        Is it like the priests'
        release in Leviticus?

The male without blemish
and dashed blood?
    The limbs in pieces?
    The tents of meeting?
        The burnt offering?
        Does it hasten deliverance?

Or summon Presence?
Is its savor pleasant?
    As the rage unfurls
    in a storm of flame
        and the darts deploy
        in a shawl of pain,

does it soar like *justice*?
Contain a God?
    Expose a Source?
    What will is known?
        Does it touch *a throne*?
        Can we see a crown?

As the swarm scorches
the air with anger,
    and the torches of righteousness
    extend their reach—
        What power is power?
        Whose heart gives out?

When skin is *pierced*
to receive that flight,
    what light gets in?
    What's left of sin?
        What cause is served?
        What cry is heard?

When the blood of infants
and elders spurts
    across T-shirts
    does it figure *forever?*
        As it wreaks its change
        and seeks *revenge*

above the *abyss?*
Could Satan devise
    vengeance like this—
    war which is just . . .
        an art of darkness?
        Have mercy, skies.

                        Jerusalem, The Gaza War, 2014

IT'S IN ME

struggling,
strangely, I feel it,
rustling, smoldering,
hollows enfolding,
something forming,
feathers rushing
through sheaths beneath
thickened skin,
buds pushing
(like nibs on pens
from within)
then piercing it,
like spirit, always
about to be
expressed, like genius,
Novalis said,
heart's sense—
and calamus—
hooked, ribbed,
lifting toward
the aether, the body
barely, a tether. . . .

WHAT THE BEARD SAID

Smallness of mind, the xenophobic
mystic muttered, his beard a cloud,
a little too proud, I thought, hearing:
Smallness of mind—it's what makes us
miss the greatness
                              of straits opening
onto a faintness (call it largesse)
of first things' traces linking long
trails of being,
                        tales of longing,
marrow in the narrow bone
of and through our rendered listening:
low—today, for instance—skies
the winter tint of tarnished vintage
silver in a kitchen drawer.
Drawing's goyish,
                            said the cloud—
though you love it, over paths
you're always walking, wherever you are
(when you're able) spokes poking
out from the crown of cones or corners
you've never seen but seem to turn
within, within you.
                              Time and again.
Misanthropy's end, the cloud sputtered.
Smallness of mind. Magnitude's friend.

AUGUST

homage to Morton Feldman—
"before the oracle, with the flowers"
    I KINGS 7:49

1.

Here in the gloaming,
a wormwood haze—
the "m" on its head,
a "w," amazed
at what the
drink itself does:

Vermouth,
god bless you—th.

2.

What really matters now is begonia,
he thought, distracted while reading——
their amber anther and bone-white petals
missing from a jade pot
by the door—not a theory of metaphor.

3.

In this corner, sweet alyssum.
And beside it fragrant jessamine.

Almost rhyming scents in the air—
a syntax weaving their there, there.

4.

Erodium holds
an eye in the pink
looping the white of
its tendering cup.

5.

The blue moon opens all
   too quickly and floats
   its head-
          y fragrance over
             the path
     before us:

And so we slit
its throat, like a florist.

6.

These hearts-on-strings
   of the tenderest green
things that rise
from dirt,
then fall
     toward the floor,

                        hang
                in
          the air
       like——

       hearts-
on-strings of the tenderest
green things—
          they rise from dirt
then fall toward
          the floor,
       hanging in
                the air like——

                these
hearts-on-strings of the
tenderest green things,
                        rising
from dirt then falling
toward the floor,
          hanging
       in the air like

7.

Moss-rose, purslane, portulaca
          petals feeling
       for the sun's
light or is it
only warmth
or both

(they need
to open)

an amethyst
        almost
see-through
shift

8.

Bou-
        gainvillea
lifts the sinking
spirit back
        up and nearly
into a buoyancy—
        its papery
pink bracts
proving with
their tease
        of a rustle and glow
through the window—

there *is* a breeze.

9.

Epistle-like chicory
blue beyond
the bars of these
        beds suspended

in air,
(what doesn't dangle?)
elsewhere, gives
way to plugged in,
pez-
     purply thyme,
against a golden
(halo's) thistle.

10.

What's a wandering
Jew to you
two, who often do
wonder about
that moving about?
Its purple stalk
torn off and stuck
elsewhere in
the ground takes root
and soon shoots
forth a bluish
star with powder
on its pistil.
Such is the power
of that Jew,
wherever it goes
(unlike the rose),
to make itself new.

NOTHING HAS TAKEN ME

Nothing has taken me
    more by surprise—
        that dove, cooing
            on a branch between
            the islet and river,
        its collar pistachio
    green, its breast
lapis, its neck
ashimmer, its back
    and the tips of its wings
        maroon. Its ruby
          eyes had flitting
          lids of pearl
    above, flecked
and bordered with gold.
Its beak was black
at the point alone,
    a reed's tip
        dipped in ink.
            The bough was its throne.
           It hid its throat
        in the fold of a wing—
    resting. Moaning,
I startled it. And seeing me
weeping, it spread
    its wings, then beat them—

and as it flew
    it took my heart
away. It's gone. . . .

Abu al-Hasan 'Ali bin Hisn,
Arabic, 11th century

WHERE THE LEMON TREES BLOOM

Jerusalem : Promised Land : Palestine.
Could words give off a greater shine?

But *no country*, he scrawled, *will more quickly dissipate*
romantic expectations . . .—which is to say, its fate

awaits the anticipation. In particular, Jerusalem
can sicken. Herman Melville, eighteen fifty-seven.

THE UNSURE MORALIST

I'm tired of life and its troubles.
Whoever lives as long as I have or will
grows weary: it's inevitable.

I've seen the fates trample
the young in the dust, like a blinded camel.
When they strike they can maim and effectively kill;

when they miss— men live on, content if feeble.
A man's true nature in time is revealed,
no matter how hard he tries to conceal it.

I know what's happening now quite well,
and I clearly hear the past's babble.
As for what tomorrow will sell us—

my wisdom's already rubble.

Zuhayr, Arabic, 6th century

WHAT THE BEARD SAID, II

What does it mean that a name remains
unknown to one who'd bear or bears it
with pride in its bearing
                    a strange sort of power,
if not exactly
                    glory? How would it matter
that an unknown name's rearranged, continually
within a body, maybe
                            anagrammatically,
as bursting books and bookshelves groan,
like someone's God?
                    Whose meanings might
that not quite grasping
                            come between—
        letters rattling
around in a skull and clicking through limbs,
                as though through limbs?
Or—Ezekiel's living beings
        racing down a thought's crown
toward the feet of what's been called
the Queen, or just a beanstalk?
                            And so from the ears
a beard, as the Brightness brings it,
brooding
            into a reading
descends and encircles the mouth—
                    white strands branching

into paths of an odd enhancement, black
waves winding their weirder
and weirder maze around and past
what we trust
            or might begin to
spell or fathom—alone with a name
                   we think
in part   we hear
but on our own could never utter

OPEN FOR BUSINESS

1.

Not to see through a scrim—
   though maybe in a simulacrum.
   Not to list or listen
   one's way into something that might have been.
   Not to live in abstract deferment
   but only to sound the lines we're in—
   the music their graphing makes, regardless
   of where that takes us, say,
   into a space where I've been remiss,
   or others dismiss.
      Always to stay open for business.

2.

Always to stay open for business
   in this *isness*, no matter the mess
   one stumbles into. Whatever the mask
   one's face is strung through.
   There *is* a blessing in this being
   not just you. Eventually. It's also true,
   you do want to become who you are,
   or at least be seen as such—
   although it might not take you far.
   Still, this much we can try to do
      for you. Now. Whoever you are . . .

3.

For you, now, whoever you are,
   hovering in your penumbral nature,
   shimmering in the pitch of address
   to yourself as someone else:
   Sounds aren't strung along the lines
   of thinking, so much as thought's defined,
   for an instant, by a sense—
   this one sinking   into your voice
   and leaving you nothing in the way of choice
   except to shout out from a crouch that
      you've assumed in the face of assault.

4.

You've assumed in the face of assault
   that in fact it's not your fault.
   Sound did it to you—listening.
   Laboring, well, the minute particulars
   of cadence and pitch and intonation.
   A surface tensility akin to a quality
   or texture combining with taste in the mouth,
   suddenly altering the air in your ear.
   Actually, that would be fear speaking
   from within, which only goes to show you
      that everything out there is also an inkling.

5.

That everything out there is also an inkling
   isn't something I'd been thinking of—
   but here it is inside my morning,
   linking things without my knowing,
   or really trying to. An inkling isn't
   only within, or even mostly.
   Nor does it really involve any ink,
   beyond the letters you're blinking at now.
   Often it feels like it's trying to figure
   its way out of a certain darkness.
      At times it even counts as distress.

6.

At times it even counts as distress
   when what's withheld should be about,
   but isn't. Or, when what's ever-so-vaguely beyond
   is something we've desperately tried to possess.
   Mostly that wanting is what defines us,
   and words manage our restlessness.
   They're what we do our wanting with, said the
   therapist, strumming our interest in all of this.
   In all of this, there's something humming,
   like an engine that needs—not to be fixed,
      only adjusted, for time's nicks, and tricks.

7.

Only adjusted for time's nicks and tricks
   can one really be seen to be someone,
   by which I mean: the Many makes us
   the one we're becoming. And aren't. It takes us
   through whatever we were, and possibly past
   what we might have turned into. And, thank the gods
   of our fathers' mothers, or their brothers'
   family trees—it seems to shake us
   out of its sleeves. So everything feels
   at once both given and chosen. And this, too,
     is one of those tricks that the Many can do.

8.

Is one of those tricks that the Many can do
   something you might try at home
   on your own? Don't be foolish.
   Tricks will happen in any event,
   without your having to do a thing,
   but pay attention, which seems like everything.
   Then again, they rarely occur
   unless your focus is elsewhere—not exactly
   on vacation, but, for instance, facing
   a deep blue dish with a Fasi pattern,
     encoding a faith in fate's sleight-of-hand.

9.

Encoding a faith in fate's sleight-of-hand
    seems like a disciplined sort of insouciance.
    It *has* produced, at any rate, extraordinary
    faience. Candy for the eyes of some,
    for others— a metaphysical emblem. . . .
    Like these lines, you might be thinking,
    with them, if everything's coming along
    as I think I'd like it to. Now there's a pause
    in the composition   a waiting for a second
    wind, or inspiration—something to do
        with paradox riding its cause into song.

10.

With paradox riding its cause into song,
    what—ducking, as he said it—he mused,
    could possibly go wrong? And when it did,
    he'd chalk it up to the greater gear-work
    of Lady Wisdom's endless lessons,
    in which whatever would be would
    always—maybe—be for the better.
    Such was the mystery of her linking letters.
    But in that *possibly*—was it true?
    The summer's rubble filled with children.
        Where was Lady Wisdom then?

11.

"Where was Lady Wisdom then?"
    is something Job's readers have wondered,
    finding her blurred among his friends,
    abused and elusive in their vapor.
    Though what she knows goes right through them.
    She's like a poem, not some palm
    marking the start of a kind of oasis,
    akin to an answer that one might have missed.
    She weighs amazement with all that is—
    and sees us   back into the welter and gist
        of a being always open for business.

SOUNDS IN THE GRASSES

The Rabbi opens a verse in the Radiance:
   The letter is small, the fullness of all.
The Sound's wind adjusts the miscanthus.
   And paper once was made with piss.

The letter is small, the fullness of all
   the grasses might just also teach us.
That paper once was made with piss
   I read in the paper before I wrote this.

The grasses also just might teach us
   behind the house, if not in Genesis.
The paper I read before I wrote this
   is a touchscreen lit by circuits and chips.

Behind the house, let alone in Genesis,
   how does value in a word seep through us
(from touchscreens lit by circuits and chips,
   which likewise involve an economy of piss)?

How, in a word, does value seep through us?
   Again I turn to a verse in the Radiance,
which likewise involves an economy of piss:
   Rabbi Isaac is nearing Tiberias—

I'm turning again to a verse in the Radiance—
    a catbird is singing from the tasseled birches—
and Rabbi Isaac's nearing Tiberias
    might be a word's trying to reach us.

A catbird sings from tasseled birches.
    Isaac thinks of the Tree of Life.
A word might be trying to reach us
    by the arbor vitae's branchlets. Through the dust,

Isaac is thinking of the Tree of Life—
    as a full-moon maple glows in the garden
by an arbor vitae branching from dust:
    I'll place my dwelling in your midst.

As a full-moon maple glows in the garden.
    And there it is, deep in Leviticus—
That *place . . . my dwelling . . . your midst.*
    Small comfort, the grasses teach us.

FOR A THEOPHORIC FIGURE

Allen Grossman, in memoriam

(1932–2014)

Strange how first things dawn on us
    late in the game,
                    again and again.
Just last week, for instance,
                I learned
of a young man's lines that appeared on a page,
black flames on a blaze of white—
    early June,
           the year I was born:
The bell pursues me, they said, *it is time . . .*
    to sigh in the ears of my children.
                  They did,
and do still, though their maker has died,
    and I, a scribe to that living word
he carried toward his distant God
    across diasporas of imperfection,
try now to lift it ever
    so slightly higher, or longer on high,
to honor,
              as I'm able, that force
    he rode for the span of more than his life
out of the Eden of his mind like a river. . . .

WRITING ON THE WALL

We hurl ourselves over
    then over again
into the wall
    of the invisible,
or walk to where
    we think it is
and run our hands
    along it as if
it were braille
    to a better being—
welling between
    all we're nearing,
now as anger,
    now as patter,
now as weather
    or someone's skin,
soon as water—
    say, the Aegean,
glaucous above
    an abyss within.

"HAVE YOU SEEN THE RAIN?"

Have you seen the rain? We are calm.
Three angels from an ancient story
are moving slowly between the trees and homes.

Nothing has changed. Only the rain
is carefully hitting the stone. The street is glassy.
We see how three angels are crossing
the street from an ancient story.

The flour is pure. The door is open.
The rain is quiet. The miracle has already happened.

Leah Goldberg, 20th century

THEY'VE GONE

They've gone on to their world—
and that is all their world,
but here my heart's devoured
by hunger for this world:

to hunger for its hunger,
be satisfied by its thirst,
to grow within the growth
of its seed and root—

to love it now,
and now despise it,
but to be within
its ardor and its fear.

Leah Goldberg

ON GIVENNESS

What if givenness *isn't* enough—
and the wind's slithering along my arm
is really a subtle summery alarm
trying to tell me something else,
and much rougher?
     That worth, for instance,
depends on a violence of difference,
      and therefore
inevitably lies at a certain distance
from the stuff of life and us?
That even givenness has to be taken
hold of,
   at least by a kind of frame—
if not a reaching for steeper comparison?
And here it is,
    as though it were kissing
the thinnest of skins on my arm, or name.

II

Translations: Late Antiquity

TO RISE ON HIGH

To rise on high
and descend below,
to ride the chariot's wheels
and explore in the world,
to wander on earth
and contemplate splendor,
to bask in the blessing
of the Crown
and sound Glory,
to utter praises
and link letters,
to utter names
and behold what is
above and below,
to know the meaning
of the living
and see the vision
of the dead—
to ford rivers of fire
and know lightning.

Anonymous, Poems of the Palaces, Aramaic

FROM WHOSE BEAUTY THE DEPTHS

When one stands before the throne of glory,
he begins reciting . . .

King of kings . . .
                    encircled by braided branches of crowns,
encompassed by branching commanders of radiance—

who covers the heavens with wings of his Splendor
and in his majesty appears on high;

from whose beauty the depths are lit,
whose glory flashes across the sky—

proud envoys shoot forth from his form,
powerful creatures burst from his brow,
and princes flow from the folds of his robe.

All the trees rejoice at his word
as the grasses delight in his joy—
and his words pour forth as balm
in flames of issued fire,

proffering pleasure to those who search them
and peace to those who make them live.

Poems of the Palaces

HYMN TO THE HERALDS

You who cancel decrees and unravel vows,
    remove wrath and bring fury to failure,
recalling love and friendship's array
    before the glory of the Palace of Awe—

Why are you now so wholly fearful
    and now given over to gladness and joy?
Now so strong in your exultation,
    and now overcome with terror?

They said: When the wheels of Majesty darken
    great dread and fear overwhelm us—
and when the glow of the Presence appears
    we soar in tremendous bliss.

Poems of the Palaces

EACH DAY

Each day as dawn approaches,
the King sits in majesty
and blesses the holy creatures:
To you, my creatures, I speak,
before you I declare—
Creatures who bear the throne of my glory
with all your heart, and willingly with your soul—
Blessed is the hour of your creation,
and exalted is the constellation
beneath which I gave you form.
May the light of that morning continue to shine
when you came into my mind—
for you are a vessel of my desire
prepared and perfected on that day.
Be still, creatures of my making,
so I might hear my children pray.

Poems of the Palaces

FROM **THE BOOK OF CREATION**

Twenty-two letters to start with.
He engraved, quarried, and weighed,
    exchanged and combined—
and with them formed all of creation
and all that he was destined to fashion.

Twenty-two letters
carved through voice,
quarried in air,
and fixed in the mouth
    in five positions:
certain sounds in the throat,
certain sounds on the lips,
certain sounds against the palate,
and certain sounds against the teeth,
and others along the tongue.

Twenty-two letters fixed
in a wheel like a wall
with two hundred and thirty-one doors—
    the wheel whirrs
    back and forth. . . .

How did he
combine, weigh,
and exchange them?
Aleph with all
and all with Aleph;

Bet with all
and all with Bet.
Over and over and on again,
through two hundred and thirty-one gates—
with every creature
and also speech
issuing from a single Name.

He created substance from Nothing—
from absence making *what there is*—
He hewed tremendous columns
out of air that can't be grasped,
seeing, shifting,
and fashioning
all of creation
and every locution
within a single Name,
and the sign
bearing its witness is:
twenty-two figures of longing
in a single body bound. . . .

Anonymous

A BYZANTINE DIPTYCH

I. ON WHAT IS NOT CONSUMED

"And the angel of the Lord appeared to him
[in the heart of the flame]"
EXODUS 3 : 2

Angel of fire devouring fire
Fire Blazing through damp and drier
Fire Candescent in smoke and snow
Fire Drawn like a crouching lion
Fire Evolving through shade after shade
Fateful fire that will not expire
Gleaming fire that wanders far
Hissing fire that sends up sparks
Fire Infusing a swirling gale
Fire that Jolts to life without fuel
Fire that's Kindled and kindles daily
Lambent fire unfanned by fire
Miraculous fire flashing through fronds
Notions of fire like lightning on high
Omens of fire in the chariots' wind
[Pillars of fire in thunder and storm]
[Quarries of] fire wrapped in a fog
Raging fire that reaches Sheol
T[errible fire that Ushers in] cold
Fire's Vortex like a Wilderness crow
Fire eXtending and Yet like a rainbow's
Zone of color arching through sky

II. LEVITICUS AGAIN

"And his issue is unclean"

15 : 2

He is human and so will be humbled
He is flesh and so will fail
He is bone and so will be broken
He is blood and so will bleed
He has cheated and so will be changed
He has deceived and so will be drained
He has mocked and so will be muddied
He is hollow and so will howl
He has sullied and so will sadden
He is nothing and so will be nought
He is pain and so will perish
He is emission and so will be missed
He is water and so will weep
He is cavernous and so will cry
He is dross and so will disgust
He is a carcass and so will be cast
He has soured and so will stink
He is rank and so will retch
He is a worm and so will writhe
He is corruption and will be betrayed
He came forth, and so he will fade

Yannai, c. 6th century

III

The Invention of Influence

(2014)

ON BEING PARTIAL

I'm partial to what's possible,
he thought—not the ineffable,
distant, devoid of insistence
and temperament that tampers,
or tramples
        Not the impersonal,
but that which hovers here—
between the "I" of the opening
and the "us" of your possible listening
now, or in the imperfect
tense and tension of what
in fact articulates the eternal
That abstract revelation
and slippery duration
to which, it seems, I'm given
and because of which I'm never
finished with anything, as though living
itself were an endless translation

SONG OF THE SHATTERING VESSELS

Either the world is coming together
or else the world is falling apart—
    here—now—along these letters,
    against the walls of every heart.

Today, tomorrow, within its weather,
the end or beginning's about to start—
    the world impossibly coming together
    or very possibly falling apart.

Now the lovers' mouths are open—
maybe the miracle's about to start:
    the world within us coming together,
    because all around us it's falling apart.

Even as they speak, he wonders,
even as the fear departs:
    Is that the world coming together?
    Can they keep it from falling apart?

The image, gradually, is growing sharper;
now the sound is like a dart:
    It seemed their world was coming together,
    but in fact it was falling apart.

That's the nightmare, that's the terror,
that's the Isaac of this art—
    which sees that the world might come together
    if only we're willing to take it apart.

The dream, the lure, isn't an answer
that might be plotted along some chart—
    as we know the world that's coming together
    within our knowing's falling apart.

QUATRAINS FOR A CALLING

Why are you here?
Who have you come for
and what would you gain?
Where is your fear?

Why are you *here*?

You've come so near,
or so it would seem;
you can see the grain
in the paper—that's clear.

But why are you here

when you could be elsewhere,
earning a living
or actually learning?
Why should we care

why you're here?

Is that a tear?
Yes, there's pressure
behind the eyes—
and there are peers.

But why are *you* here?

At times it sears.
The pressure and shame
and the echoing pain.
What do you hear

now that you're here?

The air's so severe.
It calls for equipment,
which comes at a price.
And you've volunteered.

Why? *Are* you here?

What will you wear?
What will you do
if it turns out you've failed?
How will you fare?

Why are you here

when it could take years
to find out——what?
It's all so slippery,
and may not cohere.

And yet, you're here . . .

Is it what you revere?
How deep does that go?
How do you know?
Do you think you're a seer?

Is *that* why you're here?

Do you have a good ear?
For praise or for verse?
Can you handle a curse?
Define persevere.

Why *are* you here?

It could be a career.

Azure lobelia props up the heart
   that extra hair's breadth happiness is.

———

Gray ashes, containing lashes,
   in a tin can is his father.

———

Lavender leaves are *not* lavender.
   And then the spike of its pistil climbs.

———

Sepia tilts the actual into
   the light of a slightly milder notion.

———

Umber always hovers under
   the red of whatever gets said.

———

Zaffer's not saffron—it's cobalt,
   circling back to the azure start.

FROM **ACTUAL ANGELS**

"And Jacob sent messengers":
Rashi stated, actual angels.

1.

Are angels evasions of actuality?
Bright denials of our mortality?
Or more like letters linking words
to worlds these heralds help us see?

3.

Gone is the griffin, the phoenix, the faun.
Only angels in the poem live on

as characters catching the light between things,
as carriers of currents from the wings

of thinking we know where we're going and then
getting somewhere, despite our intention.

4.

Maybe an angel's confused with an angle
so often because the slip lays bare
something these envoys are trying to tell us—
that what we're missing is already there.

5.

The light off the Sound this morning
is like the sound of the morning's light—
a high-pitched, crisp, silvery ping,
though not of burnished wings, touching.

6.

Angels also act like classics,
tilting us toward the oddly real—
as with the crust of their reputation,
they block off access to it as well.

7.

How is it that creatures with names like Anáfiel,
Shakdehúziah, Azbúgah, and Yófi'el
could possess the power to raise a person
up to a Temple-within from his Hell?

8.

Angels are letters, says Abulafia,
in us like mind as the present's hum.
No one knows what a year will bring,
but the world-to-come is the *word* to come.

12.

The elm slides liquid leaves through its sleeves—
its twig-tips swell with a ruby-like glow;
seraphs of jade then crown this mage,
their wings spreading the shade we know.

16.

We're getting closer to understanding
how angels slip inspiration by us:
science shows its wing-like spikes in
the superior interior temporal gyrus.

18.

Enoch ascended to heaven and saw
seraphs posted at fiery stations,
encircling I-AM's Palace of Awe.
All this—by means of translation.

19.

What the day is spelling out
recalls, in its way, revealed scripture
concealing the real, as the Psalmist says:
He turns the wind into his messenger.

MORE FOR SANTOB

(de Carrión, Castile, 14th century)

1. EVERYONE'S SO HIGH

Everyone's so high on "Yes."
Nothing has made me happier, though,
than the day I asked my lover if
she had "another"—and she said "No."

2. SPELL IN PRAISE

A choir of quatrains
   in praise of the servant
who asks of me nothing
   for what he does.

For years he's afforded me
   spectacular favors,
as though in fact he
   served out of love.

He somehow bears—
   though slight in stature—
the weight of the world
   within his words,

and blind he sees
    what I hold in mind;
deaf he absorbs
    what I've not yet heard.

He knows what I want
    before I've spoken,
and without speaking
    says who I am.

And so I've done
    as my debts demanded,
and sung for this spell
    in praise of the pen.

3. HOW FRIENDS ACT

Is anything better
than a pair of scissors,
which separates those
    that separate them?

They do this not
because they're bitter,
but out of desire
    to meet again.

When they're joined,
they do no harm—
hand to hand
    and lip to lip;

only when parted
can they destroy—
that's how strong
    their loyalty is.

Those who'd learn
what brotherhood means,
and how friends act
    when all is done,

should watch as scissors
make one of two—
and when they have to—
    two of one.

4. FOR BEING BORN

For being born
on a bush of thorns
the rose is certainly
    worth no less—

nor should wine
be scorned that's fine
but comes from lesser
    parts of the vine.

The hawk is likewise
no less blessed
because it was born
    in a humble nest—

and proverbs aren't
less noble or true
for being spoken
by a Jew.

BEING LED

As I write I'm being led
by matter older than I am
(but from the place where I was born)—
a yellow pencil on which the words
Again the Leader—
                    1946 Chevrolet,
Paterson, N.J.
        have been engraved.

The eraser, however, is less
than useless
(using it only makes matters worse
and blurs what appears on the page).

It surfaced somehow not long ago:

I found it among my father's papers.

The pleasure it affords is strange.

FROM THE INVENTION

OF INFLUENCE: AN AGON

Part One

The following considerations are based upon a single example of the "influencing machine" complained of by a certain type of schizophrenic patient.

VICTOR TAUSK, VIENNA, 1919

It's a machine, said the doctor,
  of a mystical nature—
reported on at times by patients.
  Their knowledge notwithstanding,
witnesses are able to offer
  only the vaguest of hints
as to how the air loom functions.
  It makes them see pictures. It produces
thoughts and feelings, and also removes them,
  by means of mysterious forces.
It brings about changes within the body—
  sensation and even emission,
a palpable kind of impregnation,
  as one becomes a host.
For some it's driven by faint effluvia
  derived from human breath;
for others electric charges are sent
  directly into the brain.

It's born of a need to explain the cause
    of things inherent in man.
Certain factors are always involved:
    Enemies. Displaced erotic
tension. Boundaries are called into question
    as though one's thoughts were "given"
and knowledge implanted from beyond—
    so what's within is known.
One does nothing on one's own.
    Strings are pulled and buttons
pressed, all to evade an anxiety
    that rears its head at the heart
of the void in avoidance. The echoes begin:
    The cure as illness, the illness
as cure. Thus the revolving door
    that becomes a lament for the makers—
and for those who fall prey to the powers—
    of this most intricate machine.

                            ———

"By three things
                the world is hung"

—is strung among the Fathers' Sayings

(absorbing them we become like sons).

So this is among the sayings of the sons—

Without these things
　　　worlds are expunged:

　　　instruction is one,
　　　　　　devotion another,
　　and the constant bestowal of kindness

　　　is the third
　　thread said the father who'd serve

in the warp and weft of daughters and sons

———

That I am a son, said Tausk,
　　around the time he encountered Freud,
　　　causes me great embarrassment
(it shames me)
when someone calls me by the name
　　handed on by my father . . .

because a father conceived me
and a mother brought me into this world.

Destiny's what the eyes can see,
the ears take in, the hands contain—
still we're called to account with the elders,
and blood misled, misleads again.

And so with a needle he pierced

that picture's heart—
his mother

on the wall

———

No one will tell you, they said, about Tausk . . .

Victor Tausk—

2.

It always begins
with simple sensations
     of change within
harmless at first,
then coupled with
a sense of estrangement

without awareness
of a source
     in control
and then with one
within oneself
but not oneself

In the case of Miss N. it appeared
to be wholly beyond her,

somehow like
a silk-lined coffin
   containing another,
but with a head that might be hers—

as though the dead were speaking,

or something dormant in her

———

What is instruction? asked one son.

Instruction is knowing—
not just what it *means* to be One,
but how to know how that needs to be done.

And what is devotion, wondered another.
Devotion is slaughter, a rabbi answered,
    of self in prayer like a fledgling dove,
    of self in the service of what we love.

And kindness?

Kindness said one
from the town of my fathers—

Kindness links worlds—below and above.

———

Miss N.'s invention was wholly hostile;
but at the heart of the art it involved,
it would be fair, said Tausk, to equate
the machinations of love and hate.

3.

"He saw a skull floating by on the water"

(water bearing the fathers and sons):

Hillel the Elder (father unknown)——

You drowned others and so were drowned,
and those who drowned you in time will be drowned.

The skull is Pharaoh's, said one of the sons
of the sons, and who,
　　　　　　　said another, drowned him?

　　　　　　○

A third rabbi demurred:
the skull floating by was a friend——

and one of the sons of the sons of the sons
thought of the father's saying:

　　　"Know where it is you come from
　　　And where it is that you're going
　　　And before whom you will stand"

———

but everyone knows
what I'm thinking,
   or what I've discovered
      they've long known

because they set it
out for me,
      because it was set
out for *me*—

the language we speak—
the language we seek—
is the language spoken
our words emerge
from beyond
(within)

our innermost thoughts are foreign,
implanted with great cunning

Thus the outer
      world of the inner
world that all can see

and that inner world of what's beyond me—

it shames me

———

"Among the sacrifices . . .
                 we must count
Dr. Victor Tausk," wrote Freud,

"this rarely gifted man,
a Vienna specialist in nervous diseases

who took his life
before the peace was signed."

4.

I have no right
    to act as I do,
        it isn't my business
            to seek new paths,
but to provide for my children.

"Tausk is a man like any,"
said a friend, "who has to do his duty."

How deeply his words have touched me.

Touched me as catastrophe.

Why shouldn't I
    try— I
haven't really tried
anything
in my life—

he wrote his wife
        at twenty-six,

    a father of sons
(1906).

Instead I've been pressed
into a mold.

———

What would be is calling
  with voices like those
of shy children,
  a barely conceived
will to survive,
  to live, to thrive
faint through the din
of the clanging day.
These are inklings,
  kin to what
one might become.
And yet, the waves
  at times close in,
and what is shy
  begins to die;
one sees it there
in eyes
    greeting others
as though they were searching
for brothers. . . .

———

Said one of the sons of one of the fathers,
  in the name of Eliezer, and others:

Set your brother's honor as yours—
  within your name, feel his shame;

and be not easily angered
  anger coils in the hearts of fools;
The day before you die repent—
  which always might mean now;
Warm your blood by the sages' fire—
  the tongues of which light worlds before you;
Beware, though, of their glowing embers—
  lest you be burned by wanting to know;
for their bite is the bite of the fox—
  whose tricks will rip through flesh;
and their sting is that of a scorpion—
  with pain so keen it sings;
and their hiss is the hiss of the serpent—
  the saintly, too, have their venom;
and all their words are fiery coals—
  with flames that, flickering, lick and maim.

7.

April 1908, he writes:

We muster a tentative Yes to our life,
unsure of just how much we can give.
Little by little we master our doubts
and begin addressing ourselves as a friend.
Gently fill the bowl to the brim,
or rather, let the bowl fill.
The task is to carry it, full, uphill.

———

There's a strange step
behind the door—
It fills me.
I hear it all.

I feel the coldness of the wall.
The handle turns . . .
And between the door and jamb,
a strange face—like mine . . .

Vienna, 18 February 1909

8.

Let the dead be.
Let them rest.

The dead won't ever
have to race
or shuffle through filth
and shame again,

or seek to suck
salvation from heaven.
The dead don't ever
have to listen.

This isn't religion.

The dead won't wake
with a morning's fright—
no ancestors come
to rebuke them at dusk.

Let them rest.

But if it turns out
that you're derived
from the dead
whose messengers arrive—

if you're driven—
don't render your life
more difficult still
(or your dying).

If you've been chosen,
don't resist.
Let them be.
It's good to rest

and see what they see.
Let the dead be.

Part Two

Now what is going to happen
only Freud and God know....
TAUSK, SUMMER 1909

Invention isn't god-like:
   it doesn't create out of nothing.
It works through what's found: it discovers,
   and much like influence, it recovers

a charge that's already there,
   potentially, in the air.
All bodies are capable
   of being (mechanically) thrown

into a state in which
   they're said to be *electrified*.
Francis Hauksbee, the Elder,
   England, 1706,

constructed what's now known
   as an Influence Machine.
A crank turned a spindle,
   which rubbed insulated matter

against a spinning globe
   of glass—an emptied vessel
really a vacuum chamber—
   filled with mercury vapor.

The friction caused a shift
   and transfer of such force
along a conducting body—
   it took on a luminous glow

inside that bordered void.
   The glow of life, some called it,
shimmering like a TV.
   And so power could be

sent through a person's hand
   or room, and then across
the spinning globe, giving
   light to a body by it.

In these Orbs of matter,
   Hauksbee observed, *we have*
some little Resemblance of the Grand
   Phaenomena of the Universe. . . .

What looks like nothing—holds everything,
   including a warning to all
would-be inventors: Remember—
   machines of this sort aren't toys,

and they're dangerous when mishandled.
   A basic contraption comprising
a charged pint-sized capacitor
   can incapacitate, or kill.

3.

He left an uncanny impression, said Freud,
who felt the disciple somehow in him,
thinking his thoughts though out ahead of him,
under his skin. Whose ideas
were *his*? What sort of sympathy was this?
Something deeply familiar, but strange,
which rendered one oddly at home in the foreign,
and also alien to what one had been.
Where would it take them? What could be known
on one's own? Weird is the word
that suited him: as in what was destined.

———

Talk about strange—in a haunted way:
    Tausk recently told me,
reported Lou Andreas-Salomé,
    how after times of strong

intellectual productivity
    which had been ended forcibly
by a distraction from without,
    though possibly from within,

he would become acutely aware
    of certain lines and forms.
He could stare at the leg of a table,
    an S-shaped ornament's curve,

as though that swerve suggested a whole
    world of inner relations—
as though he'd observed, at one and the same
    time, all that had gone

into bringing them into being
and found there boundless joy and fulfillment.

———

Precisely this
    afflicts the plagiarist,
or something like
    the X he is:
What's old and has
    long been known
seems to him new
    and becomes his own.
He's all reception,
    all alone,
and the fruits are manifold
    though the root is one—
thwarted ambition
    and a sense at heart
the doctor describes

as a kind of cry:
I cannot bear
    not to have been
the first to have uttered
    a certain thing.

———

Freud said he could never be certain
in view of his wide and early reading,
whether what seemed like a new creation
might not be the work instead
of hidden channels of memory leading
back to the notions of others absorbed,
coming now anew into form
he'd almost known within him was growing.
He called it (the ghost of a) cryptomnesia.
So we own and owe what we know.

———

"From the first stirrings of the dream," wrote Lou,
"through to the place where we're fully conscious,
    we are only en route."
And this too—
    "Poetry is something between the dream
        and the reading."

Which might be just: Poetry is something between . . .

———

To be a link
to something more

and in that thinking—
to know its core.

4.

The great Talmudic sage Eliezer,
before he became a rabbi and master
and said all he said he'd heard from his teacher,
was hungry and wanted to learn. He was twenty-
two years old, the son of a farmer
he told he was leaving the land to study
in the city, though he wasn't ready.
His father forbade him from tasting food,
and leaving, until he had finished plowing
a long furrow filled with stones.
Then he was gone. Such was his hunger—
he still hadn't eaten—that while he was walking
he picked up a stone to put in his mouth.
He'd eaten dirt all his life.
Eliezer was hungry. The son of a farmer
unfed by his father's furrows and future.
He reached an inn and spent the night.
At dawn he went to Ben Zakkai,
famous already as Wisdom's father,
and sat at his feet, there in the dust.
A stench wafted up with his breath.
"How long has it been, my son, since you've eaten?"
Silence. He asked him again; and again
nothing. And Ben Zakkai taught him:
"Only when hunger becomes insufferable

not just to oneself, but to others,
will it bear fruit it doesn't devour.
As the odor is rising from your mouth,
so your fame for learning will travel."
And he would confess, a lifetime later—
"A single dog can lick from the sea
more than I've managed to take from my teachers."

5.

I was engaged to a Christian—
Tausk wrote in a split
case of a case study—
unwilling to convert,
and so was obliged to adopt
her faith to marry. Our sons
by this marriage were baptized.
In due course we told them
about their background, lest
they be swayed by views
at school. Once at a summer
house of a teacher, in D.,
while we were sitting at tea
with our friendly hosts—
who hadn't an inkling of
our ancestry—the teacher's wife
took up a pointed attack
on the Jews. Afraid of the awkward
exchange that would no doubt ensue,
and alarmed at the prospect of ruining
our trip, and losing our lodgings,
I held my tongue, and listened.
But fearing my sons in their candid
way would soon betray
the truth, I tried to send them

out of the room, but slipped,
and instead of saying "Go
into the garden *Jungen*
(young ones)," I said *Juden*
(Jews). The courage, it seems,
of my convictions had broken
through. And the subterranean
faith of our fathers, I found,
could not simply be
dismissed as chance, since one
is always another's heir
and might in time become
a harbinger of one's own.

———

New façades and prim homes
show us no more than color and form,
not what's living, lurking, within.
Concealed things, Tausk told Lou
(1912, mid-December,
as the two were drawing closer),
are best revealed by those Jews
used to viewing ancient rooms
through the scrim of crumbling ruins.

———

We held within us dark forces
(Freud said of a friend he'd miss)
inaccessible to analysis—
that something which is most mysterious
and makes the Jew just what he is.

6.

We do live through more than we are, wrote Lou.
Or are we more than we normally live through?

○

Freud on Tausk, to Lou one night
after the break with Jung, his "son,"
on why, for now, Tausk was the right
man to have at hand: "He's clever
and dangerous. He can bark *and* bite."

———

Only now do I perceive
the whole tragedy of Tausk's situation,
Lou suddenly sees in her journal—
1913, late summer:
He'll always take on the same problems
and tackle the same lines of attack
Freud takes up, never creating
room for himself. It isn't chance.
It indicates his making of self
a son as violently as he hates
the father for this configuration.
What he wants is blind and dumb

self-expression. Suffering so
under the burden of his own person.
And this as well: Perhaps a certain
hole in creativity is filled
through that murky identification
with the father (as the son),
which in time yields the illusion
that he's achieved the exalted fusion.

———

I.M.——an Influence
    Machine, in short;
and we are what we
    become in its import.

o

The Invention of Influence?
    I can hear the sigh
as it's reduced to
    the I of I.

———

Then she spoke of maternal being—
his, although it wasn't in him—
between the beast of his daily prey
and his precious self-dissolution.
It's all so painful to see, she said,

that one would rather look away,
or flee. It's himself he's deceiving
with his fantasies. Something wraith-like
and impure resonates through him, buzzing,
as though with murmurings from within.
And yet, from the very beginning
she understood that it was true—
it was the struggle in him that moved her,
"that of the Brother-Animal—You."

Part Three

"I am allowing this horsecart of fate
to run across me," he wrote from Lublin
as chief physician at the wards,
where, in September, he was stationed.

"We shall see with what a skeleton
I'll start a new life after the war."
Thus Tausk to his ex-wife,
living in Zagreb with his mother

because she'd run out of money and sent
the boys away to school as boarders
until their troubles might subside.
1916, six months later,

his father died: "Peace to this
much-tested man," he wired home,
as though he were writing his own eulogy.
He began writing of war symptomology—

peasant conscripts who took on the look
of sad and sick domestic animals,
others wound with convulsive tics,
adrift, as he put it, in "twilight states";

a depressed paranoiac calls out—"Sir,
I wish to report that I am a deer,"
having been shot like a buck as he leapt
from tree to tree, fear to fear.

He tried to spare men execution
for turning their backs to rubrics of duty
defined in terms they'd never known—
patients bound by law to join

"in the destruction of human beings
and human value, people shipped
like ammunition to their ruin.
I began this work with the greatest aversion,

having escaped sitting in judgment
of others when I was younger and served
before and over the courts of the Law;
but now I must account for myself

with this insight whose worth is greater
to my country in the end
than the death of a few malingerers.
Forgive me," offered the difficult doctor—

a charismatic and chronic deserter
of others, said some, and his own nature,
"for shielding a boy who would not slaughter
a shackled group of enemy prisoners

or one overcome as if by forces
from without—though speaking through him;
and restless wandering fugitive souls
in petty flight from paternal compulsion,

or frightened flight from impending madness,
or noble flight to a flimsy ideal—
driven by sickness-for-home run amok,
swirling like eidolons of the real;

however decrepit and wretched they are,
fleeing while betters are being condemned—
without pity, to manure the soil
with their flesh and with their blood—

these too merit the mercy
of a Law that looks within the son
and sees the wound the father inflicted
causing infantilized soldiers to run—

men no worse than many others . . ."
(Tausk closed his "serious survey,
with serious words spoken in jest")
". . . who also evade the general suffering

and cannot renounce their gratification,
and fill their heart's desire like children,
and whom the term deserter would honor—
because they live on *profit* from war."

○

He acted, wrote Freud, in his obituary,
heroically—throwing himself wholeheartedly
into exposing the many abuses
that doctors committed or feebly excused.

2.

1918, late December—
Freud refused him
    analysis with
the father he'd master
    within the disaster
he'd always almost
    just become
(his trouble with love
    in particular
being what he'd
    hoped to discuss).
"A dog on a leash"
    is what Tausk was,
he told a colleague
from their circle,
    "he'll eat me up";
instead he referred him
    to a disciple,
his analysand—
the bridge between them
    a woman again.

For twelve weeks
the two considered
Tausk's response

to the refusal:
his grieving sense
    of dismissal at heart,
and paranoid notions
his thoughts were being
    somehow sifted
by the Master
(whose thinking he was).
    And still his self-
sufficiency drew him,
always that distant
    presence within.
His analyst's sessions
    with Freud, in turn,
were given almost
    wholly over
to what Tausk told her
    during their hour.

Then they were done.

————

Whoever possesses *my mysterion*,
    a rabbi recorded, is my son.

o

Eliezer once defied the majority
    and God on high took his side,

sending His voice down from heaven.
The rabbis, however, quoted the Deity
    to himself, Deuteronomy 30:
        It (the teaching) isn't in heaven!
And the Lord laughed with joy and replied:
My sons, he cried, have defeated me!

———

Tausk's task
    was simple enough:
become the aggressor
    by being crushed,
and be a good son
    by committing the sin
of dying to show
    what the master was missing.

———

He liked to liken his students to dogs
taking a bone from the table to chew it
    in a corner, on their own.
        But, he'd note, it is *my* bone.

———

March 26, to Lou once again
in Göttingen:

"Freud shows respect,
   but little warmth.
Nevertheless,
our relations are better
   now that I
seek them no longer.

Much better
they cannot become.
But I've at last
been cured
   of my
   desire for them."

3.

"Lieber Herr Professor," he writes
to his teacher three months later,
assuming a casual form of address
and asking the master to please excuse
his absence from the evening lecture.
"I," Tausk announced, "am occupied
with the decisive affairs of my life
and do not want by contact with you
to be tempted to seek your assistance."
The tone was odd, the language awkward—
Tausk's—but somehow altered. "I hope
to soon be free," he adds, "to approach you,"
noting that he planned "to appear
with a minimum of neurosis."

———

Later that night,
        the early hours:

Lieber Herr Professor,
Please render assistance to my
     beloved fiancée, Miss Hilda
Loewi (II Kornergasse 2),
     the dearest woman who ever came

into my life. She will not ask
   much of you. I thank you for all
the good you have done me. It was much—
   and has given meaning to these
last ten years of my life.
   Your work is genuine, and great. I depart
this world knowing that I was among
   those who witnessed the triumph of one
of the greatest ideas of humankind.
   I have no melancholy. My suicide
is the healthiest and most decent deed
   of my derailed existence. My heart
holds no resentment. I accuse
   no one of anything. I'm only dying
somewhat earlier than I might have
   died naturally. . . .
      I greet you warmly—
                  Yours,
                     Tausk

Please, also look after my sons
from time to time.

4.

Then he was gone,
gone but there,
   a corpse in the air;
a crater punched
   in his head by his gun,
he hanged from a cord
as a carcass is hung.
Now he was no one—
"the father of im-
   purity's fathers"
is what the fathers
called a cadaver;
   and yet, at last
(within the chain
   of his tradition)
Tausk had become
   more than he'd been
and spurned all along.
Peace to this man,
   this much-tested son.
Now he was one
who'd speak from beyond.

5.

1 August   Dear Frau Andreas
    (Freud writes), Poor Tausk,
    whom you favored with your friendship
    for some time, took his life
    on 3.7. He had returned
    worn out from the horrors of war
    and was intending to remarry,
    but reconsidered (so F. put it).
    What was behind it we cannot guess.
    He spent his days wrestling with
    the father-ghost. I confess,
    I do not really miss him. I've known
    for quite some time that he was useless—
    and, indeed, a future threat.

        Once or twice I had the occasion
    to glance at the foundations on which
    his high-flown sublimations rested . . .
    and long ago would have dropped him,
    if *you* had not raised him so
    in my estimation. . . .

        For my old age I have chosen
    the theme of death. I've stumbled on
    a most remarkable notion, rooted
    in my theory of the instincts,
    and now must read all sorts of things

new to me but pertinent to it.
I am not fond, however, of reading.
With warmest greetings,

                              Yours,

                                        Freud

6.

That a son can't bear his name is a shame, or a sham,
like one who's not quite his own man
(a sun with a "u"—to a larger system).
A son with an "O" of address, or an "o"—as before
the "h"—of a sigh, says I am only I in relation.
And yet, sons make a nation.

Sons for some are angels,
for others baubles, or squinting infants,
a kind of endorsement,
or not what was meant. Or a torment.
A grown son referred to as such, it's true,
is often a kind of embarrassment.

One son is said to be God, or God's.
Another's merely a mother's deity.
A son is a link in a chain that links, like a gang's,
or a tutelary. Being a son involves a bond
or being bound. It's a tie that blinds and defines.
That keeps one in line. At times it's like wine,

but then it's a chink in the good old armor.
The favorite son is often a charmer.
A son might marry the farmer's daughter
and have sons or a son's daughters.
Certain sons are marked for slaughter.
Once a son, always a son, even when one is a father.

But sometimes a son is a *door* to the father.
And then that son's seeing is double,
and so he believes that relation is noble
and the sole source of becoming singular
so as to matter, somehow, to others.
Thus a son gives birth to his brothers.

That a son is a name, then, isn't a game,
though it is up for grabs. And that's not a shame,
it's a tradition. A son's an emission.
Desire's expression. A bearer of cues, and clues,
a spooked thing—and maybe an influence, or just a fluency,
demanding or dormant, through you, through me.

WHAT IS

For *MRM, in memoriam*

The Norway maple's chartreuse crown
in April ciphers autumn's flares,
startling with mace-like spikelets of flowers
swelling over the paths of that square

where we wander, adrift in the branching—
or is it what's branching adrift in us—
wafted as if afloat on a wisdom
flowing through this city forest.

The grid encodes an understanding:
Those who stroll past tines of elms,
who'll wade the shade of summer's linden
and trace the mottled bark of planes,

move as though of their own accord
but under invisible gates of a grace
born in their being borne along
or gradually dying to the spell of the place

where dogs are walked and judgment is rendered
and power, as weakness, brings down limbs;
where mercy's continual averment is tendered,
and children at recess dart into rings;

where a woman's will surges through her
sitting alone in the rinse of her cancer,
as the vapor of chatter's released to the air.
All part of the terrible splendor—

the weeping cherry shedding petals,
like snow in an ancient ocular rhyme—
the sight, of course, is a site of convention,
the tiniest of triumphs over time,

and yet—somehow, the sarabande combines
as majesty. The rupture and gentle carriage
of kindness. The wind's extended winding
kiss. The almost now actual: a marriage

not so much of opposites as,
say, analogous aspects—exits
to entrances, or attics holding an axial
weave of sound's foundation. The praxis

perfecting opens into. An instant's
happiness putting us back in the business
of funneling the whole shebang, which Kabbalists
have given a name. Kingdom. What is.

IV

Translations: 11th Century

GAZING THROUGH THE NIGHT

Gazing through the
       night and its stars,

  or the grass and its bugs,

I know in my heart these swarms
are the craft of surpassing wisdom.

  Think: the skies
      resemble a tent,
    stretched taut by loops
and hooks;

and the moon with its stars,
  a shepherdess,
  on a meadow
    grazing her flock;

and the crescent hull in the looser clouds

  looks like a ship being tossed;

    a whiter cloud, a girl
      in her garden
        tending her shrubs;

and the dew coming down is her sister
     shaking water
     from her hair onto the path;

   as we
      settle in our lives,

like beasts in their ample stalls—

   fleeing our terror of death,
      like a dove
         its hawk in flight—

though we'll lie in the end like a plate,
   hammered into dust and shards.

Shmuel HaNagid, 11th century

THE GAZELLE

I'd give everything I own for that gazelle
   who, rising at night to his
      harp and flute,
    saw a cup in my hand
     and said:
"Drink your grape blood against my lips!"
   And the moon was cut like a D,
     on a dark robe, written in gold.

Shmuel HaNagid

THE APPLE

I.

I, when you notice,
    am cast in gold:
the bite of the ignorant
      frightens me.

II.

An apple filled with spices:
    silver coated with gold.
And others that grow in the orchard,
      beside it, bright as rubies.

I asked it: Why aren't you like those?
      Soft, with your skin exposed?
And it answered in silence: Because
    boors and fools have jaws.

Shmuel HaNagid

FROM ON THE DEATH OF HIS BROTHER

I.

A brother is in me
     whose letters
   were like water
when my heart was thirsty.

Now, when others' come,
   not his,
the thought of him writing
    within me is fire.

II.

A psalm to the hearer

of prayer in my spirit forever.
    To praise him is proper
       who metes out justice
    to the children of men,
like the sun for all revealed in its sky.
All who govern hard in their power,
   first he created youthful and soft,
     like grass and like labor,
       and the poplar and oak.
But grief he created strong in its birth,
     and weak in its growth,

and wherever it festers
in a thinking heart—
heart is lost.
From God-without-name to people is grace
neither language nor speech can measure.

I'd said in my mourning despair
would quickly wear through my heart
which, like an alley,
had narrowed with worry,
but now with solace is wide—
and my sorrow sheds
like the flesh of my brother.
If my heart is stirred and at times I weep,
and the sadness still rises within me like hosts—
more often than not I'm calm like a man
whose heart is empty,
his burden light.

So the Rock wounds
and then heals the stricken.
May he who blankets the sky with night,
and wraps my mother's eldest with dust,
forgive my brother his errors—
and in his grace remember his goodness—
and with our fathers
who were pure and his treasure,
count him as treasure.

Shmuel HaNagid

FROM *AFTER PROVERBS*

I'D SUCK BITTER POISON

I'd suck bitter poison from the viper's mouth
    and live by the basilisk's hole forever,
rather than suffer through evenings with boors,
    fighting for crumbs from their table.

FIRST WAR

First war resembles
    a beautiful girl
we all want to flirt with
        and believe.

Later it's more
    a repulsive old whore
whose callers are bitter
        and grieve.

IF YOU LEAVE

If you leave a
long-loved friend
    today in disgust,
you'll be like a man
destroying a building
    that took him a year
    to raise from dust.

YOU WHO'D BE WISE

You who'd be wise
should inquire
    into the nature of
        justice and evil

from your teachers,
seekers like yourself,
    and the students
who question your answer.

WHEN YOU'RE DESPERATE

When you're desperate ride
        the lion's back
    to sustenance,
but don't use others
    or envy them—

    the envy will weigh on
    your heart, not theirs.

IT'S HEART THAT DISCERNS

It's heart that discerns
    between evil and good,
so work to develop your heart.

How many are there
    who heartless destroy,
and think their destruction a start?

WHO WORKS AND BUYS HIMSELF BOOKS

One who works
    and buys himself books,
while his heart inside them
        is vain, or corrupt,

resembles a cripple
    who draws on the wall
a hundred legs,
        then can't get up.

WHAT'S FAMILIAR

What's familiar is sometimes distanced,
    and the distanced sometimes brought near—
and the cavalier rider in fetlock-deep water
    who falls finds it up to his ears.

HE'LL BRING YOU TROUBLE

He'll bring you trouble with talk like dreams,
    invoking verse and song to cheat you;
But dreams, my son, aren't what they seem:
        Not all the poet says is true.

Shmuel HaNagid

THE MARKET

I crossed through a market where butchers
hung oxen and sheep side by side—
there were birds and herds of fatlings like squid,
their terror loud
as blood congealed over blood
and slaughterers' knives opened veins.

In booths alongside them the fishmongers,
and fish in heaps, and tackle like sand;
and beside them the Street of the Bakers,
whose ovens are fired through dawn.

They bake, they eat, they lead their prey;
they split what's left to bring home.

*

And my heart understood how it happened and asked:
Who are you to survive?
What separates you from these beasts,
which were born and knew waking and labor and rest?
If they hadn't been given by God for your meals,
they'd be free.
If he wanted this instant
he'd easily put you in their place.

They've breath, like you, and hearts,
which scatter them over the earth;
there was never a time when the living didn't die,
nor the young that they bear not give birth.

Pay attention to this, you pure ones,
and princes so calm in your fame,
know if you'd fathom the worlds of the hidden:
THIS IS THE WHOLE OF MAN.

Shmuel HaNagid

FROM *AFTER ECCLESIASTES*

MULTIPLE TROUBLES

The multiple troubles of man,
  my brother, like slander and pain,
amaze you? Consider the heart,
  which holds them all
in strangeness, and doesn't break.

LUXURIES EASE

Luxuries ease, but when trouble comes
people are plagued for the wealth they've accrued.
  The peacock's tail is spectacular—
but it weighs him down on the day he's pursued.

ON COUCHES STRETCHED OUT

On couches stretched out at the treasury,
where the guards' vigilance knows no relief,
you fell asleep without fear by the window
  and time came through like a thief.

YOU MOCK ME

You mock me now in your youth
  because I've grown old and gray;
I'm old, but I've seen the carpenters
  building their coffins for boys.

WHY REPEAT THE SINS

Why repeat the sins
    you know will make you sad
and not hold back from sinning
      for sorrow—

like a dove whose brood was slaughtered
    in the nest, and yet returns
      over and over again
        until she's taken?

KNOW OF THE LIMBS

Know of the limbs embroidered with dust
    and covered with ashen skin,
and in these graves see the power of kings
    reduced to the powder of bone.

You whose souls on earth were exalted
    will soon rise over all—
and be remembered in the world ever after
    as a dream as it fades is recalled.

EARTH TO MAN

Earth to man
    is a prison forever:

These tidbits, then,
    for fools:

Run where you will.
Heaven surrounds you.
Get out if you can.

Shmuel HaNagid

TRUTH SEEKERS TURN

Truth seekers, turn to my poems
    and you who are ignorant, learn:

they'll teach you hidden wisdom
    and instruct you in all that's arcane.

Don't fall for words that are empty and vain,
    but hold to these poems and you'll hold to faith.

For the weak poem kills the soul of its author,
    while he's still alive, it dies—

where the excellent in memory endures,
    like the new moon, month by month in its rise.

Shelomoh Ibn Gabirol, 11th century

THE GARDEN

Its beads of dew hardened still,
    he sends his word to melt them;
      they trickle down the grapevine's stem
        and its wine seeps into my blood.

The beds blossom, and open before us
    clasps of their whitening buds,
    sending a fragrance up to our faces,
      as we wander out to the myrtles.

As you go, each flower lends you a petal—
    a wing so you won't crush it;
    and the sun's face glows like a bride
      whose jewels shine in her glow.

Through its circuit, daily, she glides,
    though no one at all pursues her—
    and so we think it a king's chariot
      drawn by galloping horses.

As it passes over the garden you notice
    the beds now coated in silver,
    and then when the day declines it lines
      their border with a shimmering gold.

In its sinking, soon, you find yourself thinking
    it's bowing, before its Maker;
        as it swiftly sets it seems to be veiled
            in darkening red by the Lord.

Shelomoh Ibn Gabirol

WINTER WITH ITS INK

Winter with its ink of showers and rain,
with its pen of lightning and palm of clouds,
    wrote a letter of purple and blue
      across the beds of the garden.

No artist in his cunning could measure
    his work beside it—and so,
      when earth longed for the sky
it embroidered the spread of its furrows with stars.

Shelomoh Ibn Gabirol

THE ALTAR OF SONG

Your answer betrays your transgression,
your words are empty, your verse is weak—
you've stolen a few of my rhymes,
    but your spirit failed: you're meek.

Try taking on wisdom's discipline,
instead of poetry's altar and pose:
for as soon as you start your ascent,
    your most private parts are exposed.

Shelomoh Ibn Gabirol

HEART'S HOLLOW

And heart's hollow
    and wisdom is blocked;
    the body apparent
        but soul obscured:
    those who wake in the world
        for gain come to corruption.
On earth a man rejoices in nothing. . . .

The servant, soon, will slaughter his master,
the handmaidens turn on their mistress and queen;
a daughter will rise—against her own mother,
    a son—against his father's name.
        My eye in the world dismisses
            what others most love,
        and all is labor, a ploughing for worms.
            Slime—to slime returns.
                Soul—ascends to soul.

Shelomoh Ibn Gabirol

I LOVE YOU

I love you with the love a man
    has for his only son—
with his heart and his soul and his might.
And I take great pleasure in your mind
      as you take the mystery on
    of the Lord's act in creation—
though the issue is distant and deep,
and who could approach its foundation?

But I'll tell you something I've heard
and let you dwell on its strangeness:
    sages have said that the secret
      of being owes all
to the all who has all in his hand:
He longs to give form to the formless
    as a lover longs for his friend.
And this is, maybe, what the prophets
meant when they said he worked
      all for his own exaltation.

I've offered you these words—
now show me how you'll raise them.

Shelomoh Ibn Gabirol

BEFORE MY BEING

Before my being your mercy came through me,
    bringing existence to nothing to shape me.
Who is it conceived of my form—and who
    cast it then in a kiln to create me?
Who breathed soul inside me—and who
    opened the belly of hell and withdrew me?
Who through youth brought me this far?
    Who with wisdom and wonder endowed me?
I'm clay cupped in your hands, it's true;
    it's you, I know, not I who made me.
I'll confess my sin and will not say
    the serpent's ways or evil seduced me.
How could I hide my error from you when
    before my being your mercy came through me?

Shelomoh Ibn Gabirol

THREE THINGS

Three things meet in my eyes
    and keep the thought of you always before me:

the skies,
        which make me think of your Name,
    as they bear faithful witness for me;

the place where I stand,
           which brings my mind
    back to the land you extend beneath me;

and bless, my soul,
        my Lord at all times
    for heart's reflection within me.

Shelomoh Ibn Gabirol

YOU LIE IN MY PALACE

You lie in my palace on couches of gold:
    Lord, when will you ready my bed
for the one with the beautiful eyes you've foretold?
      Why, my fine gazelle,
    why do you sleep while the dawn rises
        like a flag over the hills?

Ignore the mules and asses,
    and see to your guileless doe:
I'm here for one like you—and you for one like me.
      Who enters my chambers
    finds my treasure: my pomegranate, my myrrh—
        my cinnamon, my nectar.

Shelomoh Ibn Gabirol

ANGELS AMASSING

"Holy, holy, holy is the Lord of hosts,
the whole earth is full of his glory."

ISAIAH 6:3

Angels amassing like sparks in flames,
their brightness like burnished brass in their casings,
before the exalted throne in a throng
    one to another in vision turn
    to laud their Lord the Creator in longing—
O sons of strength, give glory and strength to the Lord.

Sublime creatures beneath the throne,
charged carriers encased in light,
in four quarters acknowledge your glory
    and glow in entreaty and word and awe—
    on guard over day, keepers of night—
O sons of strength, give glory and strength to the Lord.

Leading your camps and hordes they look on,
with Michael your eminent prince at the front—
a myriad chariots set to your right—
    and they gather together to seek out your palace
    and bow before your partition in service—
O sons of strength, give glory and strength to the Lord.

The hosts of the second-camp stand on the left,
and Gabriel over its army looks out:
thousands of seraphs, a tremendous force,
 together surround your holy throne—
 of-and-through fire on fire they roam—
O sons of strength, give glory and strength to the Lord.

From the third-camp's ranks there rises song
with the Lord's prince Nuriel a turret before them,
at the sound of their rushing the heavens tremble,
 in their seeking the place of I-am the Creator,
 the reward of a vision of glory and splendor—
O sons of strength, give glory and strength to the Lord.

The fourth bears witness in majestic array,
with Raphael chanting your psalms and a prayer,
they wreathe the bud and crown of power
 and the four lift in perfect accord
 hymns you inspired to stave off despair—
O sons of strength, give glory and strength to the Lord.

In trembling and fear the assembled sparks
cry out as one—their will set strong;
they plead for your faithful, a people pursued,
 and send a thunderous noise to the void,
 three times invoking your station apart—
O sons of strength, give glory and strength to the Lord.

Shelomoh Ibn Gabirol

VII.

You are the light of the upper regions,

and the eye of every soul that's pure
   will take you in—

and the clouds of sin
in the sinner's soul will obscure you.

Your invisible light in the world
in the world to come will be seen
   on the mountain of God:

You are the light everlasting the eye
   of the mind longs to behold
and may yet glimpse in extremity—

but the whole of will not see . . .

IX.

You are wise,
and wisdom is a fountain and source
   of life welling up from within you,

and men are too coarse to know you.

You are wise,
and prime to all that's primeval,
   as though you were wisdom's tutor.

You are wise,
but your wisdom wasn't acquired
   and didn't derive from another.

You are wise,
and your wisdom gave rise to an endless desire
   in the world as within an artist or worker—

to bring out the stream of existence from Nothing,
   like light flowing from sight's extension—

drawing from the source of that light without vessel,
giving it shape without tools,
   hewing and carving,
  refining and making it pure:

He called to Nothing—which split;
   to existence—pitched like a tent;
   to the world—as it spread beneath sky.

With desire's span he established the heavens,
as his hand coupled the tent of the planets
   with loops of skill,
  weaving creation's pavilion,

the links of his will
reaching the lowest
  rung of creation—

the curtain
at the outermost edge of the spheres . . .

X.

Who could put words to your power,
splitting the globe of earth in your making
 half of it land, and the other water?

The wheel of the wind you established
over the sea, which it circles in circuits,
 as the wheel of it rests in that circling,

and over the wind
 you established the sphere of fire.

 These foundations are four,
  though sharing a single foundation,
   source and font,
  from which they emerge renewed

and then through a fourfold font diverge.

XIV.

Who could fathom your mysteries
   in surrounding the second sphere
   with the glowing circle of Venus,
like a queen overlooking her armies,
like a bride adorned with her jewels?

In eleven months' time she traces her compass,
one thirty-seven of earth in its mass
   as its mysteries' initiates know.

With the Lord's will in the world she renews
   quiet and all tranquility,
   gladness and winning gaiety,
     song and wordless melody—
and the wedding canopy's joy and spell.

She ripens the fruit of the land and its wheat:

the choice fruit made sweet by the sun
and the fruit brought forth by the moon. . . .

XXIV.

Who could make sense of creation's secrets,
of your raising up over the ninth sphere
   the circle of mind,
the sphere of the innermost chamber?

The tenth to the Lord is always sacred.

This is the highest ring,
transcending all elevation
and beyond all ideation.

This is the place of the hidden
for your glory above in the palanquin . . .

You formed its frame from the silver of truth;
from the gold of mind you created its matter;
on pillars of justice you established its throne:
its presence derives from your power;

its longing is from you and for you,
and toward you ascends its desire. . . .

Shelomoh Ibn Gabirol

Things on Which I've Stumbled

(2008)

IMPROVISATION ON LINES BY

ISAAC THE BLIND

Only by sucking, not by knowing,
can the subtle essence be conveyed—
sap of the word and the world's flowing

that raises the scent of the almond blossoming,
and yellows the bulbul in the olive's jade.
Only by sucking, not by knowing.

The grass and oxalis by the pines growing
are luminous in us—petal and blade—
as sap of the word and the world's flowing;

a flicker rising from embers glowing;
light trapped in the tree's sweet braid
of what it was sucking. Not by knowing

is the amber honey of persimmon drawn in.
An anemone piercing the clover persuades me—
sap of the word and the world is flowing

across separation, through wisdom's bestowing,
and in that persuasion choices are made:
But only by sucking, not by knowing
that sap of the word through the world is flowing.

FROM NOTES ON BEWILDERMENT

I.

Translation aspires, clearly, beyond its words,
beyond what it renders, beyond even—if through—
sense, yielding, or wielding, blunders and wonder,
erasing our notion of a sacred uniqueness—
the original—as incarnation of what it heard.

XIII.

It *is* possible, the language itself insists,
or seems to: the poetry *can* come through, though only
by means of indirection. Bad translation
is like drawing a bucket from a moonlit
well, and losing the silvery shine on its surface.

XIV.

It was a golden time, said Rothko,
*for then we had nothing to lose, and a vision
to gain.* Thinking of his youthful aloneness,
he wished the graduating class, not success,
but *pockets of silence* in which to *root and grow.*

XVIII.

Always, wrote Machado, *seek in the mirror
the one who's walking beside you, the other*—
though what he meant by that mirror I've never
been sure. Clearly he meant it more than literally,
given his feel for the flowing river.

XIX.

The song, another poet sang, *has gone
out of me*, glossing—theatrically—his loss
of innocence. I, innocent, thought it
the height of profundity. Now I think his
notion of song itself may have done him in.

XXIV.

It isn't done with tracing paper. Things
signaled by words charged in a row begin
to converge, just as hope a single one
or pair might be rendered fades. So we enter
the sacred order from which translation springs.

XL.

All the rivers—it's getting somehow truer
and truer—run into the sea which is
never full, said Kohelet, the preacher,
combining, in lines as close to a sigh
as any might be, pointlessness and splendor.

XLIII.

Thus the call for kindness. The lovers' creed.
Things heard as though within one. But suddenly
freed by others' words. Nothing's original.
Not even sin. The mild wind now blowing
may be wisdom, bringing someone what he needs.

XLVI.

Lord, goes the prayer, increase my bewilderment.
Which really means allow me to question
everything, but not be lost within that
stance to the small flowers of common sense
in season. Increase, Lord, my discontent.

XLVII.

But keep me from resentment. Reason as well
has its season, although we don't believe it,
or put too much faith in it. It's true that
one and one, on occasion, is three or more.
And the middle way *is* often mystical.

XLVIII.

Lord, goes the prayer, keep me from delusion.
Which really means allow my mind to open
to all that comes my way, without bringing
ruin upon me—through fusion of things that are
distinct at heart. Keep me from conclusion.

XLIX.

While the case is being made. And the world
is all that is the case. Keep me from too much
seclusion. Increase my confusion with
Thee, it says. But is that in fact another
matter, I wondered, as the dervishes whirled?

L.

And may my love and language lead me into
that perplexity, and that simplicity,
altering what I might otherwise be.
But let it happen through speech's clarity—
as normal magic, which certain words renew.

VALENT(L)INES FOR A.

What law and power has blessed me so
that in this provocation of flesh
    I have been wedded to gentleness?

*

Delicacy of an intricate
mesh of our thought and meals and talking
    has brought me to this exaltation

of syllables and a speechlessness—
to December dusk, and desk, and skin
    in the amber of our listening.

*

Dawn again pink with munificence;
heart again blurred by its ignorance:
    toward you in that equation I turn—

and you, in turn, involve our being
spun like wool from which soul is weaving
    a use for that useless opulence.

*

Doing and making—the end served by
what it is we make, and what we do,
    is what has made me: making and you.

THE GHAZAL OF WHAT HE SEES

"If one asks, what is the Depth of Primordial Being, the answer is: 'Nothing.'"
YOSEF GIKATILLA (SPAIN, 13TH CENTURY)

What he sees when he sees—the wintered almond trees unfolding
white flames of nutrition's pistils through the blueness beckoning—

is nothing without the mind's holding it there in the day's crucible
    reckoning;
and when he considers it, that thought, too, is nothing

without the fed fire of the word's burning
into the black whole of knowing's nothing.

It's all a matter of poise in pain, or bliss: an equilibrium.
So words are uttered and sentences made, which are nothing

but a pact arrived at, a living—
a kind of suspension bridge across an infinitely wide, magisterial
    river's flotsam flowing,

cables strung and girders soaring,
as though its immeasurable mass, and freight, were nothing.

FROM THINGS ON WHICH I'VE STUMBLED

among the remains of the Cairo Geniza

Poetry and all that garbage,
   left in a pocket
     of the mind
     or a pair of pants,
       a robe,
or slipped inside a book—
    thought's *disjecta membra*—
a letter forgotten
(a recipe scribbled on its back)
a shopping list,
or bill once due,
   living's marginalia—

the rubble of what we've known was true . . .

*

In a crawl space over the prayer floor,
a storeroom perched on Coptic columns,
high in the wall of the women's gallery
(reached by ascent on a ladder only
and entered doubled over . . .)
where the legend's serpent, waiting, coils—
the words in darkness held to paper,
rags really,
    brought to light in dimness linger

as words do, as knowing is
not what's there but how we lift it
up with the winches of syntax and sense,
up in the eye of desire for linkage
of every sort, including chance—
pointing and leading through that sense,
like Keats's hand,
 reaching through the poem . . .

And in your innocence being borne—

——

With me for a moment, please . . .

——

all carried,
 into the air and on

and with all his desire brought me
and from within his heart he taught me
 my heart's secret
and so my . . . was raised,
and my eye has not grown dim

. . . was the badge
 of sense they wore
 on their sleeves
 almost thin;

beauty limned
in so many seams,
though not as gems,

but soundings within——

as his desire made me
sad before him

———

as in addition what is brought——

as in addiction what is brought——

for certain
what depends
on the wise and
worth of those who vow . . .

a hand to dig
and the ripening grain . . .

and the dove sent through the woods,

and what was ruined made wondrous again:

all of which was found
on a scrap-heap,
in the darkness,
rising through the minds of men:

Two women (twins)
found the thread
and pulled it toward them:

The wise will seek
the ancients' wisdom . . .
and keep the sayings
    of renowned men,

and enter into the subtleties
        of parables,

and search out their hidden valencies,
    and marvels,

and let their secrets speak to them . . .

    —said the linen
    rag informed
    by iron gall,
        of oak and wine—

"Do not speak about the matter
            till tomorrow.
I will come
    to you tomorrow
        about 11 p.m.,
and talk over . . .
with you
how to make the matter known . . ."

―

. . . over what remains;

so with a pact
you came, and
with a claim—
and it was kept
and then made plain.

As everything precious my eye has seen
in you came to fruition . . .

―

and there's the badge, once again
        linking beginning and end. . . .

II.

And so not just
   the names of God
      they sought to guard
from desecration
   but the forms
      composing them:
"*Letters are things,*
   not pictures of things"

—Eric Gill,
who'd reach Jerusalem.

And from the refuse-heap before him:

Five fine covers—
    one gazelle's blood red,
    one a violet that's pure,
    one the color of musk,
the others sulfur yellow and silver . . .

and eight small carpets—please,
    my lord,
the red should be as red as can be,
the yellow and white should be exquisite . . .

the gold brocade is very pretty
but not what I wanted exactly—
    for it's white and blue,
      while I had in mind an onion color,
        an open hue—
    but the lead-gray robe is superb . . .

      —

You also asked for head-scarves,
although you know what a nuisance that is—
    the souk's packed
    from dawn to dusk—
  it made me have a relapse, twice,
    but this is what I bought:

one black, with a white border
  (just as you ordered),
another azure with gold threads,
the others oak-green, cream, and red;

you asked, too, about the pearl
and the light-grayish honeydew—
    but these were mediocre,
        or over-priced,
and, I think, a waste of money . . .

thus the color-
    intoxication
that's spoken of:
the dyes extracted from nature
(brazilwood, indigo, saffron, and soot,
asparagus, kermes, and murex
mixed with mordants)
for yarn which
            was soaked in it—
transformed then on a loom—
fulled or thrown, beaten and pressed,
to make a soul or room complete
    with what their poets knew—

that beauty carried covers
more than just a flaw
    or seam in being
that lets us see
what's real,

but is itself a means
of conducting things concealed
that can't, by nature, be revealed—

thus its evocation,
its calling forth
    and lifting,
thus the rabbis' saying
a person should always be willing
to overpay for clothing,
    but not for drink and food—

thus the route
along which fabric flowed like poems. . . .

—

I also need, one Ehli wrote
to a friend along the Nile,
the collection of Ibn Khalfon's poems—
        either send it on and I
                will copy it out,
        or have it copied for me.
Please!

. . . someone borrowed . . .
    from me . . .
and took it with him
    to Yemen.

. . . don't forget
no matter what . . .

—

remember . . .

III.

Not just the past ascending into
    the present of a given seeing,
but that present itself collapsing
    into the voices speaking to it—

so that current, mixing, becomes
    duration which one, mostly, lives:
neither the *now* of a mystical focus
    nor the *then* of an ancient grudge,

but rather time itself conceived of
    as an electron cloud above us. . . .

COEXISTENCE: A LOST AND
ALMOST FOUND POEM

"And the Levites shall speak, and say
unto all the men of Israel, with a loud voice:"
DEUTERONOMY 27:14

Over the border the barrier winds,
devouring orchards of various kinds.

Cursed be he that taketh away
the landmark of his neighbor.
And all the people shall say, Amen.

The road was blocked in a battle of wills—
as the lame and sightless trudged through the hills.

Cursed be he that maketh the blind
to go astray in the way.
And all the people shall say, Amen.

The army has nearly written a poem:
You'll now need a permit just to stay home.

Cursed be he that perverteth the justice
due to the stranger (in Scripture).
And all the people shall say, Amen.

Taken away—in the dead of night—
by the secret policeman, who might be a Levite.

Cursed be he that turneth to smite
   his neighbor in secret murder.
And all the people shall say, Amen—

as peace is sought through depredation,
living together in separation.

Cursed be he that confirmeth not
   the words of this law—to do them.
And all the people shall say, Amen.

PALESTINE: A SESTINA

Hackles are raised at the mere mention of Palestine,
let alone The Question of—who owns the pain?
Often it seems the real victims here are the hills—
those pulsing ridges, whose folds and tender fuzz of green
kill with softness. On earth, it's true, we're only guests,
but people live in places, and stake out claims to land.

From Moab Moses saw, long ago—*a land
far off*, and once I stood there facing Palestine
with Hassan, whose family lives in Amman. (We were his guests
in the Wahdat refugee camp.) Wonder shot with pain
came into his eyes as he gazed across the green
valley between Nebo and Lydda beyond the hills.

Help would come, says the Psalmist, from one of those hills,
though scholars still don't know for certain whether the land
in question was Zion, or the high places of Baal. The green
olives ripened, and ripen, either way in Palestine,
and the memory of groves cut down brings on pain
for those whose people worked them, for themselves or guests.

"I have been made a stranger in my home by guests,"
says Job, in a Hebrew that evolved along these hills,
though he himself was foreign to them. His famous pain
is also that of those who call the Promised Land
home in another tongue. Could what was pledged be Palestine?
Is Scripture's fence intended to guard this mountain's green?

Many have roamed its slopes and fields, dressed in green
fatigues, unable to fathom what they mean, as guests.
And armies patrol still, throughout Palestine,
as ministers mandate women and men to carve up its hills
to keep them from ever again becoming enemy land.
The search, meanwhile, goes on—for a balm to end the pain,

though it seems only to widen the rippling circles of pain,
as though the land itself became the ripples, and its green
a kind of sigh. So spring comes round again to the land,
as echoes cry: "It's mine!"—and the planes will bring in guests,
so long as water and longing run through these hills,
which some (and coins) call Israel, and others Palestine.

The pundits' talk of Palestine doesn't account for the pain—
or the bone-white hills, breaking the heart as they go green
before the souls of guests-on-earth who've known this land.

ISRAEL IS

Israel is he, or she, who wrestles
with God—call him what you will,

not some goon (with a rabbi and gun)
in a pre-fab home on a biblical hill.

FROM **WHAT HAS BEEN PREPARED**

"The eye, it seems, hath not seen
what has been prepared
for him that waiteth for him——"

ISAIAH 64:4 (SANHEDRIN 99A)

Sounds of rain in the trees and leaves, or a sinking feeling with
the water running. In the kitchen. Kestrels screeching. Jackdaws
squawking. Overhead, just now, a plane. A tourist asking directions.
A spouse expressing discontent. A president trying to form a sentence.
A radio host from Monte Carlo. The heavenly host from a poem's
refrain. A muffled rumble behind the day: a low haze of cloudy cover.
Skin slid on a cotton sheet. A pencil's lead across the paper. Things
we own and things we don't. Things we know. A home creaking.
Blood boiling. A neighbor's door suddenly opening. The sound of
the rain giving way to snow.

*

A revelation forgotten:
the bread of proposition
set before him always,
as a holy portion,

as a perpetual debt
to him within creation.
What does *always* mean
in Israel's instigation?

Does it recognize hunger
among the other nations,
let alone its own?
Or does its singular station

excuse it now in time?
This bread which has been called
the bread of faces faces—
said Ibn Ezra—God

facing men and women
facing women and men.
A revelation forgotten.
The bread of prepositions—

of souls and objects in
relation. *And then the priests
entered bearing bread:*
for the hungry, a feast

within that sanctuary
of what is written, and wrung
into and out of hours.
And they will be known among

the nations. Justice will be
their diversion—a presence
leading up from the mouth
of malice, which has no defense

without it. And so the pact
was kept at the tent of meeting's
table. And Johanan said:
Great is the act of eating.

*

*Always an eye for the morsel. Often a lick of the local lokum, fauna
and flora. A well-cut brick. Or sky——out an open window. Always a
meal deduced from the raw——reconfigured by heat or hurt, or ice's
application. Always an eye for the hesitation, an inclination, the
national debt. Glasses a loved one's about to forget. Always a moral.
Always a plate and always motion. Always the politician's contortion.
Always a lie in the eye toward spin. Or giving something away for
nothing. Often a burnt offering and notion. Always the teaching
and instruction. Always the law and all it weighs. (Often the haze,
for days.) Sometimes it pays. Always the priestly portion.*

*

ON THE FENCE (AS BRIDGE)

Cutting the land like a local Christo.

It takes a village. Along the ridge.

*

*Bordering being and ordering skin. Quartering faith and water for
drinking, crops and bathing. Lights and nations. What's kept out and*

what's let in. A kind of equation: As without, so within. A single law . . . for stranger and citizen? Who's who kidding? Where's that mirror? So we do unto others. Once again. That all is seen and known within. Trace of the grudge and of forgiving. As the wind picks up with evening. On the island no one is.

*

An ear open, as though a funnel
to words preserved by those who've told us:
I am only ashes and dust;
I am a worm and not a man;

and Moses asking before the Lord,
What are *we?* which the rabbis heard
as *We are nothing*, and then explained:
Over nothing he hangs the world.

———

What is it that gives rise to this?
How does their vision of the ear emerge
or Sages' understanding of selves?
The listening which is Scripture's premise?

To rub its words as though extracting
juice from fruit or the spirit that shaped them?
Or Rava buried in study, distracted,
rubbing his foot and leaving a wound?

Or so to blow on the ashes one finds
until, with breath, they start to glow . . .
This too has been prepared,
and as above, so below—

Abraham, refusing plunder,
swore that *from a sandal strap*
to a thread, he'd *take not a thing*;
for which he was given the thought of heaven

along with its azure to wrap about him,
as if he were swimming in its sea,
as though he'd said, "As for me,
I am the after-taste of ashes,

I taste the dust of what has been
and *will* be"—though this is far from complacency,
note the Sages, or just humility.
This is what, they say, is given

as being's foundation, by which we exist:
Through the merit of men in a quarrel
able to render themselves as nothing—
by this alone, the world subsists. . . .

*

Radiant morning funneling blue: into the glow of evening's robes. As
though she knew what she wanted to do, or who she'd told. There are,
said the kabbalist, two hundred and thirty-one gates in the soul. But

did he mean the soul of all—or only Israel? Or maybe the Mind
they call Supernal? And gates to what? As doors to where? Make, say
the Fathers, a fence for Scripture (of which it's written: "Turn it and
turn it, all is in it"). They're making a fence to guard the future . . .
of the People, it says in the paper. And it has many gates as well.
And they too are in the soul, and of Israel. But gates to where?
Doors for whom? Under the glow of evening's robe. And into the
radiant morning blue.

THE GHAZAL OF WHAT HURT

Pain froze you, for years—and fear—leaving scars.
But now, as though miraculously, it seems, here you are

walking easily across the ground, and into town
as though you were floating on air, which in part you are,

or riding a wave of what feels like the world's good will—
though helped along by something foreign and older than you are

and yet much younger too, inside you, and so palpable
an X-ray, you're sure, would show it, within the body you are,

not all that far beneath the skin, and even in
some bones. Making you wonder: Are you what you are—

with all that isn't actually you having flowed
through and settled in you, and made you what you are?

The pain was never replaced, nor was it quite erased.
It's memory now—so you know just how lucky you are.

You didn't always. Were you then? And where's the fear?
Inside your words, like an engine? The car you are?!

Face it, friend, you most exist when you're driven
away, or on—by forms and forces greater than you are.

VI

Translations: 12th–18th Centuries

WEAK WITH WINE

We woke, weak with wine from the party,
barely able to get up and walk
to the meadow wafting its spices—
    the scents of cassia and cloves:

and the sun had embroidered its surface with blossoms
    and across it spread a deep blue robe.

Moshe Ibn Ezra, 11th–12th century

LET MAN REMEMBER

Let man remember throughout his life
    he's on his way toward death:
each day he travels only a little
    so thinks he's always at rest—

like someone sitting at ease on a ship
while the wind sweeps it over the depths.

Moshe Ibn Ezra

ON SEEING HERSELF IN THE MIRROR

I see an orchard where
the time has come for harvesting,
   but see no gardener
reaching out a hand. . . .

Youth passes, vanishing—
and there remains,
   alone,
one I will not name.

Qasmuna bint al-Yahudi, Arabic, 12th century

A RIDDLE

Evincing the infinite—
    the size of your palm—
what it holds is beyond you,
    curious, at hand.

Yehudah HaLevi, 12th century

A DOVE IN THE DISTANCE

A dove in the distance fluttered,
    flitting through the forest—
        unable to recover
she flew up, flustered, hovering,
    circling round her lover.
        She'd thought the thousand
years to the Time of the End
    about to come, but was
        confounded in her designs,
and tormented by her lover,
    over the years was parted
        from him, her soul descending
bared to the world below.
    She vowed never again
        to mention his name, but deep
within her heart it held,
    as though a fire burning.
        Why be like her foes?
Her bill opens wide
    toward the latter rain
        of your salvation; her soul
within her faith is firm,
    and she does not despair,
        whether she is honored
through his name or whether
    in disdain brought low.

Let God, our Lord, come
and not be still: Around him
storms of fire flame.

A COAT

I've got a coat that's a lot like a sieve
    for sifting wheat and barley:
at night I stretch it taut like a tent
    and light from the stars shines on me.
Through it I see the crescent moon,
    Orion and the Pleiades.
I weary, though, of counting its holes,
    which look like a saw's sharp teeth—
and dreaming they might be mended with thread
    drawn back and forth's no use.
If a fly lands there with force like a fool,
    at once it regrets what it's done:
Replace it, Lord, with a mantle of glory—
    and one that's properly sewn.

Avraham Ibn Ezra, 12th century

179

HOW IT IS

1.

The heavenly spheres and fortune's stars
veered off course the day I was born.
If I were a seller of candles,
    the sun would never go down.

2.

I get up and head to the patron's house—
    I arrive and they tell me he's gone;
and then they tell me he's sleeping,
    in the evening when I return.

Either he's out on his horse,
    or else—he already turned in.
Pity the poor creature who's born
    under the sign of misfortune.

Avraham Ibn Ezra

THREE POEMS ON LOVE FOR THE WORLD

1.

Man in his love for the world is like
    a dog gnawing on bones:
He sucks the blood between his lips
    and doesn't know it's his own.

2.

Always be vigilant not to take
anyone lightly, no matter their size—
lest you end up holding your throat
    as you gag on the smallest of flies.

3.

I'm always amazed by intelligent people
    who never consider this:
How is it that man grows so proud
when he comes from the place where we piss?

Yosef Kimhi, 12th century

SWEET AND SOUR

Gall when it helps is good,
    even if it's bitter;
but sweetness once it starts
    to harm will soon devour.
Therefore, the wise at heart
    eat the bitter that's better,
and keep their distance from
    the sweet that makes them sour.

Yosef Ibn Zabara, 12th century

COMPOSITION

I.

"Curses" composes poems like shit
    and thinks the shit in his mouth honey.
His judgment only highlights his shame:
    he's wholly exposed in his lines of poetry.
His father was always villainy's slave,
    his mother was bound to her disgrace;
both were gathered and taken up,
    their infamy left for us to face:
for the father's filth in the son can be seen—
as the stench makes it easy to find the latrine.

II.

"Curses" came and gave me his poems—
and the next day returned, and took them home.

Giving and taking, coming and going—
a dog that returns to its vomit I thought him.

Yehudah al-Harizi, 12th–13th century

GENERATIONAL JOUST

I.

Young Man:
The writer's pen across the scroll
lays down darkness in its wrath—

Old Man:
like a snake that slithers across the dust
and leaves behind it a leveled path.

II.

Young Man:
The hawk downs eagles high in the skies,
spreading its pinions against the heavens—

Old Man:
its eyes are cut from precious gems,
its flashing wings from bolts of lightning.

III.

Young Man:
The waters slowly flow in the stream,
just like delicate chains of silver—

Old Man:
and the hand of the wind like a craftsman comes
and turns that elegance into armor.

IV.

Young Man:
Hidden from men and always veiled,
the pomegranate's cheeks are just like girls—

Old Man:
once they're opened, it seems they contain
coffers loaded with gold and pearls.

V.

Young Man:
The fruit of the nut is sweet in its shell,
but until it's broken, it can't be eaten—

Old Man:
much like those who seek like fools
and learn not a thing until they're beaten.

Yehudah al-Harizi

THE HYPOCRITE'S BEARD

The hypocrite's beard has branches extending,
    just like his cant in every direction.
Its length reaches down, deep into hell,
    after it's worn itself out with exertion.
Within it small creatures are creeping about.
    Are monkeys, I wondered, also hidden
where fleas bequeath their places to lice
    and once— I saw a night-bird flying?
They told me his beard's in fact like a forest
    where all sorts of beasts and foxes have dens;
there the arrow-snake builds her nest,
    and rabbits, too, have found a haven.
All dwell there, safe and sound,
    each beneath its grapevine resting.
And their young in the shadows of fig trees are reared,
    plump and fresh, in the hypocrite's beard.

Ya'akov Ben Elazar, 12th–13th century

SPATS AND SQUABBLES

Day after day, spats and squabbles;
Time stands still, and still we wobble.

Are we alone in this torturous state?
Do *all* lovers share this fate?

"Love like a neighbor for his neighbor,"
says my friend, "lacks all savor.

Without the tension, without the tussle,
love and poems alike are dull."

Ya'akov Ben Elazar

TO WHOM AMONG THE AVENGERS OF BLOOD

To whom among the avengers of blood can I cry,
    when my blood has been shed by my own two hands?

The hearts of those who despised me I've tried,
    and none have despised me more than my heart.

The enemy's blows and wounds have been mighty,
    and none have wounded or struck like my soul.

The corrupt have beguiled me into destruction,
    but what like my own two eyes beguiles?

From fire to fire I've passed alive,
    and nothing has burned like my own desire.

In nets and snares I have been trapped,
    but nothing has trapped me like my tongue.

Snakes and scorpions have bitten and stung me,
    but my teeth bite into my flesh more fiercely.

Princes pursued me swiftly on horseback,
    but none have pursued like my own two feet.

My anguish has swelled and long overwhelmed me,
    but stubbornness brings me much greater grief.

My heart's sorrows are many—
    and greater still are my sins . . .

To whom, then, could I cry—and who could I condemn?
    My destroyers emerge from within me.

Nothing I've found in life surpasses
    seeking refuge in your compassion.

Cast your mercy on hearts that are weary,
    O Lord, my king on the Throne of Mercy.

Avraham Ben Shmuel, 13th century

THE NUT GARDEN

The Nut Garden holds things felt and thought,
and feeling for thought is always a palace—

Sinai with flames of fire about it,
burning though never by fire devoured.

On all four sides surrounded so,
entrance is barred to pretenders forever.

For one who learns to be wise, however,
its doors are open toward the East:

he reaches out and takes a nut,
then cracks its shell, and eats. . . .

Yosef Gikatilla, 13th century

SHE SAID SHE WANTED

She said she wanted to run when she saw
    the gray scattered with white in my hair:
"Dawn's already come up on your head
    and I'm the moon—you'll drive me away."
"It isn't true," I said, "you're the sun—
    and can't, by nature, hide by day."
"You've lost your power to run after love,"
    she replied. "What good would it do to stay?"
"Nothing's changed," I told her, "except
    for the gray. I've got the heart of a lion
to do your will." And she offered: "OK,
    you're a lion. . . . Then I'm a gazelle.
Would I lie down in the lion's den,
    bright gazelle that I am?"

Todros Abulafia, 13th century

TOMORROW I'LL WRITE

At night he says: "Tomorrow I'll write,"
but there's nothing at all to back up his words;
the heavens' frost laughs in his face,
and the cackling of mocking ice is heard.

Don't pride yourself on tomorrow's prize—
when you have no notion of what it hides.

Shemtov Ardutiel, 14th century

TWO LESSONS

1.

She trapped me with temptation's bread;
with stolen waters she hunted me down.
   Her angel's eyes looking at me
   were archers slowly taking aim.

Now her cheeks are the breaking dawn.
Now her hair brings evening on.

2.

In my lap—a doe,
   and in her lap—a harp;
she plays it with her fingers,
   and kills me with her heart.

Sa'adia Ibn Danaan, 15th century

PEACE BE UPON YOU

Peace be upon you—
    ministering angels,
        angels of heaven—
from the King who is king of all kings,
    the Holy One, blessed be he;
    in peace be your coming—
        angels of peace,
            angels of heaven—
from the King who is king of all kings,
    the Holy One, blessed be he.

Bless me with peace—
    angels of peace,
        angels of heaven—
from the King who is king of all kings,
    the Holy One, blessed be he,
    in peace be your leaving—
        angels of peace,
            angels of heaven,
from the King who is king of all kings,
    the Holy One, blessed be he.

Anonymous, 16th century

HYMN FOR THE THIRD MEAL

Prepare the feast
 of perfect faith,
the delight of the holy King.
 Prepare the feast of the King.

This is the feast
 of the Lesser Presence;
the Ancient Eminence and Field of Apples
 assemble with him for the feast.

     *

Sons of the Palace—
 you who yearn
to behold the radiance
 of the Lesser Presence—

be seated here
 at this Sabbath table,
adorned and crowned
 with the name of the King.

Exult in your being
 part of this gathering
among the guardian
 angels' wings,

and rejoice now
    within this hour
of favor which knows
    not what anger brings.

Draw near me here—
    see my power,
without the judgments
    of judgment's terror.

Those without
    may not enter,
for they are dogs
    of rancor and gall.

I hereby call
    to the Ancient of Days
to summon his will
    to drive them away—

for when his favor
    in this room is shown,
the husks are soon
    made null and void.

He drives them into
    holes in the ground,
conceals them deep
    in caverns of stone.

And so it is
    now and till twilight—
within the Impatient
    One's delight.

Yitzhak Luria, Aramaic, 16th century

WHY, MY DESIRE

Why, my desire, why do you always pursue me,
    and turn me, daily, into your enemy?
Why, my desire, why do you always pursue me?

Day after day you set out your snares,
    until in guile's pit you entrap me—
Why, my desire, why do you always pursue me?

You've been my enemy since I was young,
    gnashing your teeth and working against me:
Why, my desire, why do you always pursue me?

My soul sought to follow your path,
    for your hand's shadow, it seemed, would protect me:
Why, my desire, why do you always pursue me?

My eyes greeted the night with tears,
    and as you persisted, in anger you wrapped me:
Why, my desire, why do you always pursue me?

And if I imagine you'll come to save me,
    when I call on the day of distress you'll say to me:
(Why, my desire, why do you always pursue me?)

"Your words to me are sweeter than honey"
    —and so on your hook to doom you draw me.
Why, my desire, why do you always pursue me?

School of Luria, 16th century

198

IN THE VALLEY OF ISHMAEL

Through you will the blessing be brought to Israel,
    through the secret of the valley of Ishmael,
        for the redeemer has come to restore
    through the secret of the valley of Ishmael.

He said: The Lord has heard
    his servant who has served—
        He, who within him has dwelled
    through the secret of the valley of Ishmael.

The letters hold salvation;
    the jubilee freedom is his foundation;
        through sin he brought to sanctification
    through the secret of the valley of Ishmael.

He who teaches us is the redeemer.
    It's he who established the upper splendor
        in primordial space in the shells' chamber,
    through the secret of the valley of Ishmael.

The letter of Life fell in a place
    where no one dies, the Truth is this—
        and all that is good within it exists
    through the secret of the valley of Ishmael.

These things are seen as though through a veil,
and they are most abstruse as well,
but in them I have found the real
through the secret of the valley of Ishmael.

Shabbatian Hymns, Ladino, c. 17th century

SONG OF YOU

Lord of the World.
Lord of the World.
Lord of the World,
I'll sing You a little Song of You.

You-You-You

Where will I find You?
And where won't I find You?

So – here I go – You,
and – there I go – You,
always You, however You,
only You, and ever You.

You-You-You, You-You

East – You – West – You,
North – You – South – You.

You – You – You

The heavens – You. Earth – You.
On high – You, and below . . .
In every direction, and every inflection.
Still You. However You. Only You. Ever You.

You —— You —— You

Levi Yitzhak of Berditchev, Yiddish, 18th century

VII

FROM

(1998)

FROM **SPEECH'S HEDGE**

I.

The line coils seeking extension,
  seeking leafage and fruit beyond weeds,
    seeking wheat—
      whose flowers few recall.

  The line coils seeking inclusion
      beyond amazement,

the truths of attention within its law:

  The spikelets begin to bloom
    slightly below the middle of the head
      and proceed both upward and downward;
    the glumes are split by the swelling
      of two scalelike organs within them

  and echo in thought
like the new moon I wouldn't look at
    over the suburb after a storm.

  I'd deadened myself with the wood of shelter;

  with the elegant wood I'd
      deadened myself to the awn of sound,
        to the splintering pulse

and the flax in bloom:

with the dead
wood of the phonemes /*soon*/ . . .

though the poem was an altar seeking submission—

shifting attention inside the rain;

and this was the month
of the voice in the greenness burning,

of the spirit wound in its claim.

*

Words are wood for the vanished altar.

Isaac the son who brings his own kindling.

The lord protects by concealing his name,

or laughing. The line coils
escaping derision,
and coils again embracing abjection,
establishes shape charting conviction—

the sun in the sign of the Ram—

and the April moon of redemption,

of the great tabernacle to the glume and the law,
  of the barley ripening, and the spelt to come—
      as man can't live by dread alone—
      whose flowers we pay to recall.

II. "SO THE SOUL . . .

> *. . . without extending and*
> *living in its object, is dead*
> *within itself. An idle chaos of*
> *blind and confused powers."*
> —TRAHERNE

This was love in the day—

*

the eyes' ray along
  an iron rail
 laced and white as the park
  brides in their hopes and veils

guiding my climb through the air

  toward the bolted
   double doors
  and rooms below—

Siennese, or like Escher

 —so as not to slip,

over the landscape of kingdom and savior—

of blood in the alleys and open sewers,
        of summer flies and trash,
    or Melville's wash of bone,

    and hyssop fields overturned,

        or bulldozed
            groves of olive;

a fortress of knowledge and tact
    on a far-off hill . . .

    This was love
            in the will,

    the eyes' line
            along an iron rail
        laced and white as the bride's
            prospect and veil,

    guiding her climb through the air.

VII. THROUGH THE KNEES

The weft conceived
    to further abundance,

to cushion vanity's
  cost through the knees:
    the knots
of color like chaos evolved—
          the abstraction
    supple so being gives in

to spirals of evening blue

and intricate tracery
    of vines and leaves,
   carefully crossed to shroud
    and reveal

more distant pattern below.

And then,
the I's-of-it-placed,
   assumed,

and anguish entered,
   like a diphthong;

the utile brought near
　　through wastes of time and song

raising us up through labor and things

　　with no one denied:

the middle medallion pinnacled and cusped,

dependant cartouches of interior design,

　　rose and blue lamps
　　　　on a vertical axis

then a pool-blue central escutcheon
　　　　　with lotus circles
　　and arabesque trim,

　and ribboned clouds woven through.

　　A dome of thread
　　　spun from the stuff of
　　　　warmth and food—
woven by Maqsoud of Kashan, at Ardebil, 1539:

"Away from thy threshold I have no refuge.
　My head has no guard beyond this porch.

This is the work of a slave to the place set apart."

XIII. HEIRLOOM SPINES

In this Arabian skin-
    temperature wind
a coolness
holds in the wall
    closet
  with books
  carpentry frames

and plaster:

*A Thousand Nights
    and One Night*,

Hebrew poems of Muslim Spain
  and Byzantine
    liturgical Palestine;

a new English Omar Khayyam.

  I linger—
my heirloom illness a low-flame
    to liver and blood,

    my spine
      slowly fusing.

XVIII. "I SING A DOUBLED SONG . . .

. . . to the Lord
for the double miracle he wrought."
—SHMUEL HANAGID,
GRANADA, C. 1053

For the Chief Physician
   Through the Explosion
of Belief in the Cave of the Fathers:

This is what the faithful heard
   before the rounds and slaughter,
or hoped to hear in part
   when a stranger opened fire
in the floating lunar month of months
   marking the Book's revelation—
on a festival day of vengeance exchanged
   for vengeance excused,
of fasting and masks and reversal
   and wine upthroughunknowing
one's hangman from redeemer.

This is what the faithful heard
   before the issuant fire
at the Cave of What Is Doubled,
   Machpelah, from *cephel*,

or Fold, as in double or couple;
this is the cave where the peoples'
    couples were laid to rest,
the tomb of the Fathers and Mothers,
of a man who rode in a land of promise
with sorrow before him and his son at his side,
    and bound him there in belief
    before a knife and hill

then set him free to drift
    within his name,
like mercury. This is the ghosted
double cross of faith's deep grief,
of living near the drain of the altar
where slaughter in the Name
    of the One Lord—
in unknown sound and permutation—
was slaughtered in the Name of the One,
Lord,
This is what the faithful
    heard before the fire:

But as for the godless who grossly sin,
    their refuge shall be the Fire;
    as often as they desire
    to come forth from it so
shall they be restored into it. And unto them
it shall be said: Taste the fire's torment,
    with which you've dealt as lies . . .
    We gave the book to Moses

so let there be no doubt
concerning the encounter with him.
We set it up as a guidance for the Children
of Israel; is it not a guidance for them?

This in part is what the
faithful heard across their prayer,
kneeling or ear to the wall or air
    reciting Psalms
    or the Book of Surrender
to the sound of the opening fire,
an extinguisher struck and exploding
before the ritual came to an end,
    a witness stated
before the judicial commission
before the Chief Physician

who fired was beaten and torn
like an offered bird
    for the offering of peace
at the door to the Tent of Meeting.
And the priests shall dab the blood
    against the altar round about
    in an offering made by fire
of a sweet savor unto the Lord.
. . . This is the literal word
    raised to the power
    of disbelief
in the blessing beyond the eye,

in the almond budding
beyond the Holy One Blessed Be He's
   parcel of land.
This is more
than your average Lord can stand.
If I were hungry, he says,
   in the Psalmist's song
   to Asaph, number fifty
   ("Out of Sion,
the Perfection of Beauty,
God hath shined forth . . . A fire

devoureth before him . . .")
   : If I were hungry,
   I would not tell thee . . .
This is what the faithful heard
before the doctor opened fire.

XX. NEON: SCRIPTURE

Out to the vertical
   apostolic
neon LIGHT OF THE WORLD,
  dusk's jade deepened
      to blue
 with air and exhaust,
late in a day's pursuit
 of the guild taboo,
the chronically hidden from
  billboard equation and fact,
   embedded in sense;
     staking a grant
 from the dead and dead to be
  in the raveling border
   of speaking and maybe
never appeasing the hunger for seed-
  bearing word or lifting
the sprigs of syllable up in the
  mind for no one at all:

 such was the sentence
of proximate freedom to serve for the
  time being a sign.

NEWS THAT STAYS

"It's a multiday process . . .
                              Under stress,
officially MIA, with a mission. Friendly fire.
   That's not your question?
      I have a good *answer* for it.

Sorry, but we just can't discuss that,
and I can't even discuss why we can't discuss it.

Let me walk you through that decision. Unhindered:

Elite

                    Republican

                                        Guard.

Cut it off and then kill it. In my mind's eye . . . a thousand
         points of light. If you've
              got a hammer, *find* a nail.

   What the vulnerabilities are.

I'm not trying to
gaff the question. That's a service prerogative.

To classify these folks as prisoners of war.

                    . . .

Could you tell us, Pete, if the slick will spread
    and poison all the waters in the region? I
    don't think we have a good feeling for that.

Something has happened to his country
    that he doesn't want us to see.

A daisy cutter, to soften up the troops.
Just ripple off . . . into infinity!
    A new order. Tel Aviv . . . a
crematorium. We haven't yet reached, I think,
        a point of diminishing

returns. By popular demand. Mr. Ambassador,
thank you very much for your time. My pleasure."

The Gulf War, 1991

OF PIGS AND WORMS

1. ON TRANSLATION

Like a pig's snout pierced by a golden ring;
like the ministering angels sent to sing

through one's own throat of another's joy;
like a calling, in the mouth of a decoy . . .

2. ON THE PERFECTION OF STYLE

It's crucial to develop a form
to channel all that you know
and need to know, like the worm.

QUALMS: SOME PROVERBS

Are you a person of appetite?
　　Put a knife to your throat.
There at the bulge where the blade narrows
you can build your soul and its moat . . .

　　　　　　*

Better bread and a houseful of focus
than rare prime rib with your cut-throat friends.

　　　　　　*

Folly tells him: take it—
secret pleasures are sweetest;
　　but he doesn't see the ghouls
hovering there, over the hollows of hell.

　　　　　　*

Work your ground and savor your bread;
pursue the empty and empty your head.

　　　　　　*

The fool doesn't bother with erudition.
　　He's busy with Heart's exhibition.

*

He's right as he argues his cause,
till his friends come, and give him pause.

*

The lazy worker in his craft
   is corruption's brother at heart.
The sunlight descends like golden dust
and the leaves start to take it apart.

*

The bestowal of honor on a dolt
is a boulder placed in a catapult.

*

The spirit of man can heal
his most hideous disease;
   but who in public
can bear an open wound?

*

Two things are never full,
   three are never satisfied:
the circles of destruction and hell,
   and the bottomless well of our eyes.

KHARJA/CLOSURE

(Anonymous, Mozarabic, 12th century)

"Oh, I'll
love you alright;
     so
  long as you
manage to bend

  both of my
 anklets
back to the
  thin silver
earrings you gave me."

SUITE FOR SANTOB

(de Carrión, Castile, 14th century)

I'd like to speak
of the world and its ways,
  and my doubts
about it, truthful words.

*

Lacking the skill
  to make a real living,
I offer in speech
  a share of my learning.

*

I keep myself young and lithe,
but not because I'm afraid of age.
  I'm afraid of people
who'd see me and think I was wise.

*

A single wind brought down
  the magnificent tree
but the grass in the meadow softly
  bowed as it passed.

Once there was a man
  who walked around without shoes.
And then he got some shoes,
  and soon he wanted hose.

In time he got the hose,
  and then he wanted a horse,
and then he built a stable
  and went to look for straw.

Good straw proved hard to find,
  and so he bought some help.
Good help proved hard to keep,
  and cost a lot to boot.

The story, of course, goes on
  and on and on,
the gist of it being
that our man in time was ruined

by that ancient dream of shoes.

*

Son of woman, you who think
  of yourself as a shining star
and complain when you fail to get
what you want, and turn on the Lord,

and live out your life in anger,
   have you forgotten—you were born
from a meager thing, a filthy, putrid,
squirming drop of sperm? Son of man?

*

Only to read their letters,
   notes and poems,
not to see them smiling . . .
They distilled their wisdom

in writing, not in prizes . . .
   For a kind of heavenly
sense made clear, for an hour,
   deep inside us:

That's why we read the wise.

*

We were discussing pleasure
   and happiness, and the world's
mutability: Someone said the
   sage is he who knows

that the higher one falls from,
   the worse the wound;
and he who leads his life
   along the plain

fears neither loss nor pain.
  Someone else said, So
he knows it. That doesn't
  say what he'll do.

*

People are rarely speakers
  and doers; and though it's
a pleasure to give these
  proverbs voice

their echoes haunt me
  and often hurt.
I'm weak as the next, or weaker,
  when it comes to carrying

a virtue out . . . and frequently fall
  into the ditch I've written.

*

Why was the human head
designed with a single tongue
but two ears? . . . So we should speak
no more than half of what we hear.

*

Not being able to speak
　　often causes pain
in beasts; in people
the pain derives from speech.

* 　 *

The wheel turns
　　and the rich man's poor—
and the poor man's face that's glazed with mud
　　　gazes up at the sky.

* 　 *

All my life I've suffered,
　　caught between the truth
of two ideas: what's kept
　　in silence can't be held

against one—so one emerges
　　blameless, at least;
but inner speech not cast
　　in writing resembles nothing

more than an arrow falling
　　short of its target—
an awful image extended
　　to the core of one's being.

Violent or soft, the unrecorded
　　word is like an instant's
shadow, a bay's ripple, or sea's,
leaving its fading mark on us.

(TUNING) HOOKS

All the little
   links involved,
my non-existent
    psalter said—

all the little links involved
would rot away
    in precious time

and leave a taste
    in thinking's air
  a shape impressed
  like loops and hooks

in precious time

and ingrown love

all the little
   links involved

like must on feeling's tongue,

like must on feeling's tongue.

VIII

Translations: 20th–21st Centuries

BRING ME IN UNDER YOUR WING

Bring me in under your wing,
   be sister for me, and mother,
the place of you, rest for my head,
   a nest for my unwanted prayers.

At the hour of mercy, at dusk,
   we'll talk of my secret pain:
They say, there's youth in the world—
   What happened to mine?

And another thing, a clue:
   my being was seared in a flame.
They say love's all around—
   What do they mean?

The stars betrayed me—there
   was a dream, which also has passed.
Now in the world I have nothing,
   not a thing.

Bring me in under your wing,
   be sister for me, and mother,
the place of you, rest for my head,
   a nest for my unwanted prayers.

Haim Nahman Bialik

FROM THE POOL

When I was young and my days were sweet
and the wings of the Presence first rustled over me,
my heart knew longing and mute amazement,
and I sought a secret place for its prayer.
And so, in the heat of the day I'd sail
toward the kingdom of majestic calm
into the heart of the summer forest.
There among the trees of God
no echo of a falling ax was heard;
for long hours I'd wander a path
that only the wolf and hunter knew—
one with my heart and my god until,
stepping over the golden snares,
I'd enter the sacred shrine of the woods.

Beyond the veil of the leaves lay
a green island with a carpet of grass,
serene—a world unto itself,
a holy of holies among the shadows
of the forest's trunks and tangled canopies.
Its ceiling formed a small blue dome
set and fastened over the trees—
its floor was glass: a pool of water,
a silver mirror within the frame
of the damp grass, inside which lay
another and second, smaller world.
And in the middle of that dome,

and at the center of that pool,
facing stones of jacinth shone,
large and carnelian: two suns.

And as I sat at the edge of the pool
and gazed at the riddle of the twin worlds,
not knowing which was prior—
my head bowed beneath the blessing
of the ancient grove, the play of shadow
and light as one, of resin and song—
I'd feel, palpably, the silent flow
of a certain freshness enter my soul,
and my heart, thirsty for sacred mystery,
would slowly fill with quiet longing,
as though it wanted more, and more,
awaiting the epiphany of his Presence.
Or that of Elijah. And as I listened,
and my heart shuddered and nearly gave way,
the echoed voice of a hidden God
exploded suddenly from the silence:
Where art thou?
And huge wonder filled the forest,
and the oaks of God, firmly rooted,
looked on at me from within their majesty
in amazement: Who is this among us?

A silent language of gods exists,
a soundless speech of secrets, but rich
with color, the magic of shifting forms,
a fabulous spectacle. And within that language

God makes himself known to the chosen—
His spirit's elect. And the lord of the world
reflects as he will, and the artist gives shape
to the thoughts of his heart and dreams unspoken.
This is the language of vision, revealed
along an azure strip of the heaven's
expanse, and within its silvery clouds,
and nimbus massed; in the corn's trembling
gold, and the great cedar soaring;
the white wing of the fluttering dove,
and the broad strokes of the eagle's wings;
in the simple beauty of a man's back,
and the radiant look in his eye;
in the sea's anger, and its breakers' crash
and play; in the night's bounty and the silence
of falling stars; in the noise of fire
and the ocean-roar of daybreak's blaze
and dusk. Within this language, the language
of languages, the pool spelled out—for me
as well—its eternal riddle,
tranquil, and hidden there in the shade,
seeing all and also holding
and with it all always altering.
And so it seemed like an open eye
of the forest's lord—the greatest of mysteries
and the longest reverie.

Haim Nahman Bialik

A FEW SAY:

Day after day bequeaths its fading sun,
and night after night laments for night.
Summer after summer is gathered in fall
and the world in its sorrow gives song.

Tomorrow we'll die, the word in us gone.
And as on the day that we set out, we'll stand
before the gate at its closing, and the heart rejoicing—
for God brought us near—will tremble in fear of betrayal.

Day after day gives rise to a sun that burns,
and night after night pours forth its stars,
and poetry comes to a pause on the lips of a few.
On seven roads we depart and by one we return.

Avraham Ben Yitzhak

BLESSED ARE THOSE

Blessed are those who sow and do not reap—
they shall wander in extremity.

Blessed are the generous
whose glory in youth has enhanced the extravagant
                brightness of days—
who shed their accoutrements at the crossroads.

Blessed are the proud whose pride overflows
      the banks of their souls
to become the modesty of whiteness
in the wake of a rainbow's ascent through a cloud.

Blessed are those who know
their hearts will cry out from the wilderness
      and that quiet will blossom from their lips.

Blessed are these
for they will be gathered to the heart of the world,
      wrapped in the mantle of oblivion
—their destiny's offering unuttered to the end.

Avraham Ben Yitzhak

FROM YEAR TO YEAR

From year to year it grows only more refined.
It'll be so refined in the end—
she said, and meant it.

But sometimes I feel I'm drowning in time.
I get the sense all along I've been drowning,
he muttered.

That's only because you're down, she said.
It's only because you're down and you know it.

I don't know. Sometimes I think I've no more to give.
Refined, you know, isn't far from the negative.

I know, and applaud your discovery.
I applaud your eyes and their blue.
You don't leave anything after you.

And that's exactly what troubles me.
And that's what they'll say in my eulogy.
That's what I feel, exactly.

You're wrong again: you're fine. And the fineness surrounds you.
You're riding around on its shoulders already.

Be patient. It'll embrace you.
In the end, it will give you a kiss.
You know how it happens, almost like this.

Natan Zach

TO PUT IT DIFFERENTLY

Poetry chooses choice things, carefully selecting
select words, arranging,
fabulously, things arranged. To put it differently
is hard, if not out of the question.

Poetry's like a clay plate. It's broken easily
under the weight of all those poems. In the hands
of the poet, it sings. In those of others, not only
doesn't it sing, it's out of the question.

Natan Zach

WARNING

Lovers of hunting,
and beginners seeking your prey:
Don't aim your rifles
at my happiness,
which isn't worth
the price of the bullet
(you'd waste on it).
What seems to you
so nimble and fine,
like a fawn,
and flees
every which way,
like a partridge,
isn't happiness.
Trust me:
my happiness bears
no relation to happiness.

Taha Muhammad Ali, Arabic

ABD EL-HADI FIGHTS A SUPERPOWER

In his life
he neither wrote nor read.
In his life he
didn't cut down a single tree,
didn't slit the throat
of a single calf.
In his life he did not speak
of the *New York Times*
behind its back,
didn't raise
his voice to a soul
except in his saying:
"Come in, please,
by God, you can't refuse."

*

Nevertheless—
his case is hopeless,
his situation
desperate.
His God-given rights are a grain of salt
tossed into the sea.

Ladies and gentlemen of the jury:
about his enemies
my client knows not a thing.

And I can assure you,
were he to encounter
the entire crew
of the aircraft carrier *Enterprise*,
he'd serve them eggs
sunny-side up,
and labneh
fresh from the bag.

Taha Muhammad Ali, Arabic

TWIGS

Neither music
fame, nor wealth,
not even poetry itself,
could provide consolation
for life's brevity,
or the fact that *King Lear*
is a mere eighty pages long and comes to an end,
and for the thought that one might suffer greatly
on account of a rebellious child.

*

And so
it has taken me
all of sixty years
to understand
that water is the finest drink,
and bread the most delicious food,
and that art is worthless
unless it plants
a measure of splendor in people's hearts.

*

After we die,
and the weary heart
has lowered its final eyelid

on all that we've done,
and on all that we've longed for,
on all that we've dreamt of,
all we've desired
or felt,
hate will be
the first thing
to putrefy
within us.

Taha Muhammad Ali, Arabic

TEA AND SLEEP

If, over this world, there's a ruler
who holds in his hand bestowal and seizure,
at whose command seeds are sown,
as with his will the harvest ripens,
I turn in prayer, asking him
to decree for the hour of my demise,
when my days draw to an end,
that I'll be sitting and taking a sip
of weak tea with a little sugar
from my favorite glass
in the gentlest shade of the late afternoon
during the summer.
And if not tea and afternoon,
then let it be the hour
of my sweet sleep just after dawn.

*

And may my compensation be—
if in fact I see compensation—
I who during my time in this world
didn't split open an ant's belly,
and never deprived an orphan of money,
didn't cheat on measures of oil
or violate a swallow's veil;
who always lit a lamp
at the shrine of our lord, Shihab a-Din,

on Friday evenings,
and never sought to beat my friends
or neighbors at games,
or even those I simply knew;
I who stole neither wheat nor grain
and did not pilfer tools
would ask—
that now, for me, it be ordained
that once a month,
or every other,
I be given a glimpse
of the one my vision has been denied—
since that day I parted
from her when we were young.

*

But as for the pleasures of the world to come,
all I'll ask
of them will be—
the bliss of sleep, and tea.

Taha Muhammad Ali, Arabic

REVENGE

At times . . . I wish
I could meet in a duel
the man who killed my father
and razed our home,
expelling me
into
a narrow country.
And if he killed me,
I'd rest at last,
and if I were ready—
I would take my revenge!

*

But if it came to light,
when my rival appeared,
that he had a mother
waiting for him,
or a father who'd put
his right hand over
the heart's place in his chest
whenever his son was late
even by just a quarter-hour
for a meeting they'd set—
then I would not kill him,
even if I could.

*

Likewise . . . I
would not murder him
if it were soon made clear
that he had a brother or sisters
who loved him and constantly longed to see him.
Or if he had a wife to greet him
and children who
couldn't bear his absence
and whom his gifts would thrill.
Or if he had
friends or companions,
neighbors he knew
or allies from prison
or a hospital room,
or classmates from his school . . .
asking about him
and sending him regards.

*

But if he turned
out to be on his own—
cut off like a branch from a tree—
without a mother or father,
with neither a brother nor sister,
wifeless, without a child,
and without kin or neighbors or friends,

colleagues or companions,
then I'd add not a thing to his pain
within that aloneness—
not the torment of death,
and not the sorrow of passing away.
Instead I'd be content
to ignore him when I passed him by
on the street—as I
convinced myself
that paying him no attention
in itself was a kind of revenge.

Taha Muhammad Ali, Arabic

THE BEGINNING OF WISDOM

A kiss to the wall,
    to the *aleph-bet*
that hung there

and Mr. Pakh asks me:
    Still on the
aleph-bet? Still

not beyond it? No,
    not yet! The beginning
of wisdom is the fear

of Heaven: the initial
    letter, *aleph*.
The secret of secrets

in *aleph*: kisses
    to the spot
on the wall where it hung.

Harold Schimmel

The orchard extends through a heart's reach
heartscape our ease into strangeness
the deer we move toward on the road
across the quarry at the foot of the hill
we'd climbed for its summit   are still
to our slow approach   eyes angled
something a little in the shoulders turning
or a pair still at the same between-space
wandering off to a bordering
heartscape of grapevine along the path
and the ever-pubescent almonds   also the figs
could never speak with more force or more impress
all of which here we take in as if
through a straw with a swiveling movement of eyesight

Harold Schimmel

HERE

It's possible to eat
a slice of radish

on a piece of
french bread and be

happy (here) the walls
as well are set

for song I'm finishing
now a little arak

and writing these lines
wondering if in fact

it's best to start
on something else apart

from what we know
already how to do

more or less I'd
really better get going

Harold Schimmel

FROM **LOVE**

6.

Within myself I've discovered
an opening

imagine for a moment the cave
of Pan at Banyas

and was astonished
at the shiftings of meaning there

that what's wanting we call an opening

and the opening we call the past

that the past has the supple body
of a young woman

and she told me
what no one ever told me
(what I've always wanted to be told)

and as much as she told me
so the girl in me grew

deepening, and deepening, and deepening
the past

and, accordingly, the openness

and, as it were,
all became wanting

26.

My two hands compose poems,
miles of poems,

from within your body—

remember, D., the honey

in the lion's
carcass, the honey . . .

the miles
jab at the sky

stab at the clouds

tickle the stars

man's such a schmuck—

a poem stuck up God's ass—

thwarted, feasting, thwarted, feasting

Aharon Shabtai

THE PRAYER BOOK

For years I've wanted to write a prayer book.
Why? Because I've learned
that the solid hangs upon nothingness.
Because I've found that the sentence is a kind of petition.
And because I've found that in all that I've said
in all that I've said I've said only thank you.
So, little by little,
                    in fact I've written that book
and today it weighs some two hundred pounds
and soon it will celebrate its fiftieth birthday
and yesterday I bought it shoes.

Aharon Shabtai

THE REASON TO LIVE HERE

This country is turning into the private estate of twenty families.

Look at its fattened political arm, at the thick neck of its bloated
    bureaucracy:
these are the officers of Samaria.

There's no need to consult the oracle:
What the capitalist swine leaves behind, the nationalist hyena
    shreds with its teeth.

When the Governor of the Bank of Israel raises the interest rate
    by half a percent,
the rich are provided with backyard pools by the poor.

The soldier at the outpost guards the usurer, who'll put a lien on
    his home
when he's laid off from the privatized factory and falls behind on
    his mortgage payments.

The pure words I suckled from my mother's breasts: Man, Child,
    Justice, Mercy, and so on,
are dispossessed before our eyes, imprisoned in ghettos, murdered
    at checkpoints.

And yet, there's still good reason to stay on and live here—
to hide the surviving words in the kitchen, in the basement, or
    the bathroom.

The prophet Melampus saved twin orphaned snakes from the hand
  of his slaves:
they slithered toward his bed while he slept, then licked the lobes
  of his ears.
When he woke with a fright, he found he could follow the speech
  of birds—

so Hebrew delivered will lick the walls of our hearts.

Aharon Shabtai

CULTURE

The mark of Cain won't sprout
from a soldier who shoots
at the head of a child
on a knoll by the fence
around a refugee camp—
for beneath his helmet,
conceptually speaking,
his head is made of cardboard.
On the other hand,
the officer has read *The Rebel*;
his head is enlightened,
and so he does not believe
in the mark of Cain.
He's spent time in museums,
and when he aims
his rifle at a boy
as an ambassador of Culture,
he updates and recycles
Goya's etchings
and *Guernica*.

Aharon Shabtai

PASSOVER, 2002

Instead of scalding
your pots and plates,
take steel wool
to your hearts:
You read the Haggadah
like swine, which
if put before a table
would forage about in the bowl
for parsley and dumplings.
Passover, however,
is stronger than you are.
Go outside and see:
the slaves are rising up,
a brave soul
is burying its oppressor
beneath the sand.
Here is your cruel,
stupid Pharaoh,
dispatching his troops
with their chariots of war,
and here is the sea of Freedom,
which swallows them.

Aharon Shabtai

RYPIN

These creatures in helmets and khakis,
I say to myself, aren't Jews,

in the truest sense of the word. A Jew
doesn't dress himself up with weapons like jewelry,

doesn't believe in the barrel of a gun aimed at a target,
but in the thumb of the child who was shot at—

in the house through which he comes and goes,
not in the charge that blows it apart.

The coarse soul and iron fist
he scorns by nature.

He lifts his eyes not to the officer, or the soldier
with his finger on the trigger—but to justice,

and he cries out for compassion.
Therefore, he won't steal land from its people

and will not starve them in camps.
The voice calling for expulsion

is heard from the hoarse throat of the oppressor—
a sure sign that the Jew has entered a foreign country

and, like Umberto Saba, gone into hiding within his own city.
Because of voices like these, Father,

at age sixteen, with your family, you fled Rypin;
now, here in Rypin is your son.

Aharon Shabtai

FROM

Rift

(1989)

TORCHES

A night the letters fell from the wall

like startled minnows, shimmering;
their suddenly tumbling into the dark square between

shoulder and spine, shudder, and recognition of
a moment's reeling itself out onto the seam: knowing.
Rust on his tongue.   A dream.   Someone mumbling

of letting him under the wire he heard.
They led him in along the fine line he served,

where the nerve kept, exposed, a syllable-reef

of anything possible focused
there, in the shapes—

a blue spark and glow, and alien sense, like an eel.

RIFT

1.

Shrill keeks and arcs

and dusk loops
of swifts
circling,
like gnats
swarming

the highest
darts
straight across an open
space
and two,
maybe three

shoot
quickly down, drawn
each by the one
before it
but all three
by a fourth
and sixth

and tenth,
and in

       then out of the
obliquely bordered
eye-
       let the roofs
           ridge

as others, lonelier
swoop
and rise,
    easy

  in the streams and lifted   and up

    and up   their turning in and out of a
       light
         to gray

           and bright
           white
         and back

    to black—
    their suddenly
       falling
           into a flapping
           and flying off—

           and the quiet
       patch
         empty

and after
filling

with violet spreading   and deeper   and stars

Night exceedingly
clear
is almost
    blue
    almost a
black

Pillar.
The light
    trapped.
    At the very
        middle

almost an indigo
almost
not   at all.   Nobody
    said
    a word, no

one.

Audible:

                    :   at the
                                    very

marble.
Middle: I heard him

reaching.
        I saw the body
        shambled
        in metal and
                    glass

and the presence
already clinging.

Nobody said.
At
the very
letter.

I stood, watching
the-pigeon-
incredibly-jerking-its-
            head-
        back-and-
                    forth
            as it walked.

Neither
    ox nor
    lion;
no whale;
not hawk not anyone's
  eagle.

Pigeon: simpleton.

     . . .

A dawn breaking
black
     to new

over the city   the sapphire
  sheen
  on a dove's
     hackle—

  a Jew's
    village
of when

  and the moon
  thin
  where the brightness
    bends;

the whiteness gold
                paled,
         the dark
quiet
and done,

         the sun as any   and place

         wouldn't
suffice, so all
night
         a teaching the brain what it

              Us,
Abstract and
very

as whiskey.
                   All
              except what rested
                              yet
         in the zero, down

Rain, too, as a spice.
By the sound it
   hits
   in us.

Stones
wet, and sleep, strangely
   easier.

         Or, absolutely
awake to fragrance.

January.   Pressed in a
   dictionary—
      dry petals
      veined
   and their sex beautifully
   crushed
       in that

place: maroon, fuchsia, crimson.

2.

The instant that isn't
Christ,
      that won't be
   given
  to term,   that will
     surrender
    to no cross,

    to no one's
    blood
      but own.

Before the god-
     derrick
and moon— the battered,

nickel composure.

Beneath
that gray.

    The.
     Rothko.
As though he were
  caught,

descending.   She is
  one

    shade
    beside the others
       only.

No mouth.
Calling.

Beneath that
green.

Easier: his brute
idea.

At the door,

    and the greek
    stars
    pathetic as

Sometimes she
wished
he'd come
up from behind
    with
      his prick
        hard

            as
          though he'd
            touch
             her there, inside

him.

Really what he wanted was
    always
    small, always
       the palm
       at the white
of sleep,
    always the lamb
       she was.

          Really
he'd sung of what mostly
perished
    wherever he'd been,

    and what of the wolves
remained.

3.

The footsteps not for

hard
the after you the
    sudden
     roof the
       harder
words beneath it hard the face across it hard the sound
    inside that hard the always
      not
      the far the almost
        hard
        and just

          to acknowledge the always
          hard
            the ground to
              admit
              the sound
             outside

            for you the

            hard the
            hart
            the water

And which is
          wheat
and which
straw

and is it the dream
cheating
     its ruin

          and the crackling
          thorns

and stubborned,

or better the gully
     air
     for a moment
               easy?

and which is wonder.
          The noise
          now the storm
          and trees
                over the houses

      a round clock
      ticking

            late
      in a which is
      wrong

   and when illusion

of clouds
moving
    under the one
        star
quickening through it—

  blue
beneath the (closer)
dark:

    gloaming.
    The heat
        gone
  out of its
  where

and people home: the sky
fastly

blacking Sabbath and

(Behind the rain, the white
                    mist
              and winds
              starting

        a field,
        an empty
            lot—
               anemone
        scar, messageless

        red—   opening
        there

under the
black
cope and
   sake

city and
book

possibly
   again, and again
     far

A way there

and maybe
back.

Hints of
only
belonging, only
    petition.

Foxes.   Rift.   No face.

4.

        Nowoman and stars
        blinking
        out, and indigo
           climbing
           from purple behind it.

No-
woman's electrum bursting beneath.   Nowoman
and gold

    and the walls turned.

Nowoman singing the limestone
walls.
      Nowoman angling the eaves.

  She
with the slugs and mosquitoes and mint and weeds.
      Nowoman
here at the
cistern
watching the swallows

      sweeping
    the air.   Nowoman and I—

and the swallows' dusking and dawn,
keeping a Jew's
hour
    and obdurate ebb

  and song

  Nowoman and psalm.
   Nowoman
     and words
    waiting
   there
   where the black
     wires
    cross and
   slowly
   arc and scissor

a swallow's curve
and quiet, syllable-shine.

LEVITICUS

All the fat is the Lord's—

they flayed the bullock and sliced its
    flesh to pieces sized
      for the altar

  dashing
  the blood round
  and laying the wood and head
      and suet and meat

   in order
   next to the stone—

  they pinched the skull
     and crop
  from the dove

  letting its
  blood drain to a well—

fourth a
hin the offerings of wine,

 and a lamb for peace

  the goats for sin,

and the carcasses
burnt in the   dung
and skin

with hyssop
and cedar to cover the smell

———

against him;

the paint
peeled back to flax
and wood:

cloth where the
blue
had eyes,

tree where the shell
of white was arm
and body

awkwardly—

chipped
where the crucifix
was

in that
   man's nymity,

         the Book

   auric,   above—

         ———

Song the

soul set
   air
   up in the   im-

possibility of
heart the particular
                bolt

   in the

      being
      pulse the

            morning

      anything

      other than
            skies

spirit

zeroed in on
almond
literally

burr
there

the   yard sprig
defines a range the

entering

broken

started
under the day-
stars

promise

now

in the malice
affection

fear the
flaw the hope

and edge

in sound we

knowledge

and disgust with
self and knowledge,

spirit and pain—

———

The builders' crane rose mutely—

———

Or skeletal remains of a
cat on all fours in the gutter
pitched at its dying

are apse
for an eye
in the order of elements we learn
their lines in the mind as eyes
and heart
at the object
meet in the sound the bones

were finely
set   the skin
leathery across the small
potato of a skull
          stretched

          an ear
          hooked
          gently over
             and stiffened

          the pin-like teeth
          the tail no thicker
             than a large worm
                no longer

          lungs and stomach
            gone   the unclever
          spine exposed to the
          glazed sky I'd climbed that morning
          up on the leaky roof to fix it was

          surprised   the carcass
          gruesomely
               innocent there my
            attention morbid
                 perhaps
             the thing of it louder

                    and trapped

                    between symbol and perfectly
                 normal   i.e., explicable   revulsion

                    ———

To be broken or

                 gradually
given
in   to it—

        a chorus of
                    pulse,

            instance,
                up in the

                    love
                 hidden

        and denied

        destroyed

            through flesh
                and memory
            tunneling
me briefly
I

listen in-
side that
time
the light
shifts under:

a shaft
splits
and scatters
across its
range
and beyond—

hollow the
body grows
thickly
around—

soul
as echo the body
grounds

as day redeems it,

dawn   was slates
and gray panels opening

and pigeons   x-ing the sky

———

Within

that starting

the side I'm
on through a side
I'm going

towards

the skin
I'm in is the

quiet
image the
mind
as well

up in the amber
bullock and
road

out to

bus

under streetlight
flesh

is

an image of

                    fear
               across its
               struggling

          sized
          through rooms and bodies

               and beyond

                    of who

                    to the ends
                    of the altar at

                    —son that he
                    gave his only be

                         working

                    its order next
                    to the limbs

               and slowly
                    strange   to have
                                        the crop
                                   in blood

               a wind

                    as day

to be
a hin
in rooms the
            or

            ready

        opening

        sound
            among

        the invisible
        and skin
                with
                things

        steers us

        heart

and cedar to

        statice,

            cliff,

            some rusting
                cans and

. . .

bring me there through the
                              polyptych

    of shame,

    now in this car   and the spirit's

                                        trouble

        and yaw

ALPHABET

A way cut   to the letter:

the kept bud stiffening to gem,
a rose
        found in the foil
                and leaves
                behind a hedge
        at the station.

        Its strict whirl preserved
                as gift.
        Edge and place.
                Breastpiece.

Under a facet the light cracks
and scatters in on its hinge.

FROM

A Notebook for Poetry

(2013)

FROM *A NOTEBOOK FOR* POETRY

What every master of ceremonies should say as she introduces a poet: "Prepare to meet your maker."

*

Is what most people call mysticism an escape from reality or a means of entry into it with greater intensity? Or maybe that should just be this: My standard for mysticism is the same as for poetry. Does it make life more interesting, or less?

I've spent a good deal of time in and thinking about the park across the street from our apartment here in New Haven's Wooster Square, a charmed confluence of paths and patches of grass under an urban forest canopy—plane trees and assorted oaks, Norwegian maples, sugar maples, basswood and elm, tulip and even something called Kentucky coffee. There's a flow and vitality, a roughness and variety running through this place that is what every city planner worth his sketches dreams of, and I see it in both the most concrete and deliciously Kabbalistic terms— an elaborate dance of couples and groups, loners, birds and squirrels, dogs on parade, the sefirot-like network of interlocking paths. "When will the performance begin?" a woman with a small boy in her arms asked me, one Sunday morning, as I sat there taking it in.

Then . . . as the New England spring reaches the height of its softness, D. writes from Jerusalem, among other things alerting us to his new piece in the *NYRB*, which I read last night (preparing myself for re-entry into that maelstrom next month). On the face of it a review of a new book about the crisis of Zionism—which he praises but finds too mild. In fact, D.'s is a sober depiction of the moral collapse at the heart of that place that has been at the heart of my writing life for so long (and at the heart of D.'s for longer still). Not exactly news, of course, but he makes it matter anew.

That's what we'll be returning to.

*

"Life is nothing if not sacrifice"—Lionel Trilling, quoted in the same issue. One doesn't always know where the sacrifice is, what one is sacrificing, or why (and is it sacrifice if one isn't conscious of it being so?). But Trilling is right. Subtle or substantial, joyous or tragic, it's the locus of meaning in just about everything.

Bad poetry, mediocre poetry—poetry that lacks a sacrificial dimension?

And then there's Novalis: "One submits to true translation out of a kind of poetic morality, out of the sacrifice of one's own desires. . . . In the end, all poetry is translation."

*

The latter is a notion I used to resist, vigorously, but nothing now seems more vivid or truer. Think about it: A poet writing a poem is rendering experience—above all, of relation. Which is to say, of the elemental, moral, linguistic, and psychic materials that constitute our engagement with others and the world. So that Freud's question about the agon of treatment applies: What sort of "displeasure" (discomfort), he asks, is one willing to undergo in the "labor of translation" that brings these materials to the surface of one's work—the work of analysis, or poesis?

Translation in this scheme is health, not loss—not failure, but fuller life.

*

Which brings us back to sacrifice—and in my case, to Levitical sacrifice, a subject I've been circling for more than three decades now. No theory of religion or literature ever quite accounts for it. And the link between Leviticus and poetry—that's even odder. Leviticus is, seemingly, everything literature shouldn't be: it's legal rather than lyrical, technical and not dramatic, priestly instead of prophetic, and more bureaucratic than charismatic. It's primitive. It's embarrassing. Yadda yadda. Liberals don't know what to do with it. Protestants and humanists hate it. But it's one of my favorite books, and not just of the Bible. I prefer it to almost all the famous scriptural narratives, except maybe the binding of Isaac, which also emerges from a sacrificial sensibility.

What is sacrifice in Leviticus? At heart it involves the isolation of a part to stand for relation to the whole. It entails dismemberment for the sake of remembrance. In the case of animal sacrifice, especially, it gives us the visceral, cadenced, tactile record of the rites of mediation, of a mediacy that will yield the experience of immediacy. Later rabbinic Judaism translates its choreography into a daily wringing and ringing out of words through study and prayer, thought and song, wit and commentary. So that's at least part of it: Levitical sacrifice as a concrete analogue to poetry's translational ethos.

*

I used to want to make poems as though poetry or even speech hadn't existed before me. Now I work at the other end of the spectrum, making poems mostly out of what already exists, and somehow finding that fresher. More mysterious.

*

The impulse is part of *inventio*—as in discovery—the identification of topoi, or the conceptual places in which one's deep subject and style will emerge. That's what got me to Jerusalem in the first place. Why Jerusalem? Everyone asks, and then has a hard time with the inevitable answer: to re-find and refine my English through Hebrew. To reconfigure it through what lies on the Hebraic side of the hyphen of the Judeo-Christian legacy that English poetry is, and—with a combination of luck and learning—to send it toward what might turn out to be the secret places of the imagination. As a retired six-foot-four wood-chopping shopteacher friend of my family asked at the time: "You're going to Jerusalem to study English?"

In a sense, I was. And being there, absorbing Hebrew and later Arabic, rewired my notion of what it is that poems might do, how a line might unfold and be heard, how ornament works when it really does, and what it means to be original. In its various forms—including its Arabized medieval mode—Hebrew became for me what Arabic was for the Jewish poets of Spain: the way out that led, curiously, in.

*

Something useful I stumbled on this morning while looking for music that might help me work: Bach's miraculously microcosmic "Inventions," which he titled "Honest Instruction," were written for children to teach them how to "discover" the little ideas and starting points that unfold into a piece, and then to move, within exercises in counterpoint, from givenness to song.

*

An interviewer asks if my work on the *Poetry of Kabbalah* has made my faith in, and understanding of, God more real. My eyes cross at questions like that. Absolutely, all that work, all those years, deepened my understanding of the world of Kabbalah, and it strengthened my faith in the work that words do; but, no, it did nothing for my faith in the word "God," which remains almost wholly opaque to me outside the poems.

And yet, and here's the mystery, inside the poems and their translations, within their rhetorical space—it is utterly real to me.

*

"Coming out" with that anthology of mystical poetry has me in a whole new conversation, and not one I've wanted to be part of before. The public discussion of what I've always thought should be as private as sex. My sex, for certain, but also everyone else's. My spirituality? The word itself gives me the willies. And yet here I am having spent a good deal of the past fifteen or twenty years working out ways to bring across into a viable, believable contemporary English the most intimate and sometimes even erotic religious verse of the Jewish middle ages. I suppose I've always believed that the answers or, better, the responses to questions of this sort need to be embodied in action, and that the action of poems is that embodiment.

Yesterday, for instance, a filmmaker friend was over for dinner and mentioned that she found herself both drawn into and wondering what to make of the notion that the medieval Kabbalists of Palestine and Babylonia and, later on, Spain would invest inordinate amounts of time reciting novel combinations of letters and words, or deploying them in eccentric arrangements on the page, believing that doing so would open up channels to "higher" worlds and, as it were, more powerful powers. I've wondered too. Though, when push comes to shove, isn't that what I do, or think I do, when I'm reading and writing?

*

One of those things I hope I'll never get over——the combination of tenderness and penetration in the pleasure I get from our roof-deck garden facing I-95's Anthony Caro–like access ramps and the Sound beyond them. Blending the textures and shapes of grasses and leaves, stalks and flowers, their hues, and, especially, their names——alyssum, arabis, bacopa; brunnera, coreopsis, cress; chrysanthemum, clematis, convolvulus; delphinium, euphorbia, fescue; flax, gaura, lobelia; mallow, nasturtium, phlox; rubrum, salvia, and saxifrage; sisyrinchium, viola, and yarrow—— takes me, inexplicably, behind the language lobes of my brain.

*

The space between certain Hebrew poems (medieval and modern) and English-as-it-is the moment I read or remember them—— that's what I'm often writing into.

*

Readers are suspicious of wisdom poetry and of its new-age incarnation in particular. And it's hard not to participate in that suspicion, since verse that bears the trappings of "wisdom" often lacks formal, organic counterpoint, an undertow that acknowledges how things are, or feel, over time.

To wit——wit *and* lyric, mysticism *and* skepticism. They aren't at odds, at least not in me. They're more like two ridges over-looking a single valley. One can see the same landscape from each, just differently.

*

The refrain of a Leonard Cohen song on his freakishly good new album, *Old Ideas*—the man is 78—has a quarreling couple saying (singing!) to each other, at once, and in harmony, "Frankly, I don't like your tone."

That's usually the case with work that puts me off. Something tonal. If I like your tone, sooner or later I'll probably like your tenor too, or at least begin to live with it.

*

People are always saying—I heard someone yesterday say, at a gathering of writers—that among the things human beings can't live without are stories. Is that true?

I've never felt that. But song—now that's . . . another story?

*

We like to say that poetry and its translation take time. But where do they take it? And how?

Beyond the real time poetry takes to make and read, there's the deep historical time that has gone into making the tradition out of which it emerges. And then there's the time it took us to pre-pare ourselves for the reading or writing in question: the way in which time made us ready—through study and trial, resistance, hesitation or maybe precipitous action, through exposure to mu-sics and voices of various sorts, to sensual and not-quite-sensical experience, to distinctions made between cups of tea and the tiniest waver in a friend's intonation in a room or a letter, or on the phone, to weather and hunger, the timbre of pain as it registers.

All that goes into the surface tension of a poem—becomes it.

*

Working now on, or toward, what I think may be a longish poem about conduction and sonship, paranoia, tradition and the dynamic of inhabitation. One waits, or tries to wait, as with every poem, every piece of writing, until the right moment. Not sufficient knowledge (Frost—"The poet must always begin with insufficient knowledge"), but sufficient pressure. One broods and jots things down as they come. But at what point do they form themselves into figures that might become poems? Often (ideally) it just happens, but as often (realistically) there's a delicate preliminary dance and courtship, much scribbling, thinking, attraction, repulsion, and noting the irritation of obscure intuition—when to push, if ever? How hard? Where? The nudge toward form isn't the only sort of direction involved; curiosity has its own engine, and that requires fuel and maintenance as well. Now it's pleasure. Now torture. There are, to be sure, many poems that emerge in-full and of-a-sudden, and then there are those that are lost, in part or altogether, out of impatience, a starting too soon. But most wouldn't exist without the struggling. That doesn't bring one to the magic—but it might bring one to the place where the wall or floor of false or encrusted feeling gives way. And *that* drops one into the magic. Then it seems to happen all at once.

*

To be a son in psychological and literary terms is a put-down: one is overly reliant on others' authority, hasn't matured, isn't a father, or at best embodies a spirited rebelliousness. But in the religious context it's almost always a form of high praise—a door to the father: sons of God (angels); the son of God (Christ). In Jewish terms, it's the sons (the people of Israel) who are closest to the Fathers, the carriers. Hence the opening of the rabbinic Sayings of the Fathers (Pirkei Avot): "Moses received the Instruction (Torah) from Sinai and passed it on to Joshua, and Joshua to the Elders, and the Elders to the prophets, and the prophets passed it on to the men of the Great Assembly. They said: . . . raise up many disciples."

The chain of tradition as the rabbinic equivalent of Homer's list of ships, as Auden's test of one's investment in verse. Does that imply a diminishment of intensity? An enfeebling and passively derivative nature? The ethos that informs gives shape to the practice. It's fire that's passed from torch to torch. *Lampada tradam*—Lucretian runners passing on the torch of life (and learning). And *iqtibaas*—the Arabic for Quranic quotation embedded in verse, literally, the lighting of one torch from another.

*

Surface feeling-with (that reveals depths) = sympathy
Emotional feeling-with (that implies a surface) = empathy

We like to say that the latter is deeper, more meaningful; but it's the former that matters for the writer, the translator, the poet. As in von Hofmannsthal's aphorism: "Depth must be hidden. But where? On the surface."

The Möbius strip of that aesthetic—with the surface turning out to become what's within, and what's within evolving into what we face.

*

Back once again to the dust and patchwork construction, the exposed plastic pipes, raised tones, and weary hostility of our once Palestinian, now North African Jewish and increasingly ultra-Orthodox Jerusalem neighborhood, and to the grime of the run-down, battered, and tchotchke-crammed center of the city. Are its edges getting rougher or is all this time in New Haven each year thinning our skin? Then a call from a friend, and A. and I walk up several hills to a tidier and more genteel part of town: rose-filled gardens and geranium-studded municipal squares, sculptures, tree-lined streets, an early evening breeze. As though we'd crossed into Europe.

Each time we shift sides of the globe, or even sides of the city, the systole and diastole of belonging and dispersion leaves me a little dizzy, and melancholy. For some three decades now I've felt almost at home in exile and somehow in exile at home—though which is which is always evolving. And as in homes, so in poems. The heart is twisted back and forth, as if in some sort of rinse cycle, and maybe that's how it should be. This isn't just a slippery metaphysics to keep one's wings from being pinned down. It gets at something essential, perhaps what the philo-Semitic French Catholic poet Charles Peguy understood when he called "[being] elsewhere—the great vice of this race, its great and secret virtue, the great vocation of this people," the Jews. That doesn't sanction lack of attachment; it calls on us to be where we are and then some.

Tsvetayeva to the rescue yet again—"All poets are Jews"?

. . .

Modern Hebrew's first major poet, the Ukrainian-village-born and eventually Odessa-bred Haim Nahman Bialik, grasped this like few others. In a little-read essay called "Jewish Dualism," he writes of the way in which Judaism as a civilization or culture has survived precisely because of this alternating current: now the farmer, now the hunter; now the legend, now the law; now the rhythms of Nature, now of Scripture; now the (home)land, now the abstract, universal (diasporic) idea. Remove one of these poles, he says, and catastrophe will ensue.

*

Another thought about the aesthetic of conduction: Pleasure, certain psychoanalysts have noted, pleasure is experienced with the greatest intensity in the momentary dissolution of the ego, the *ich*, the I, somatically through orgasm and socially and emotionally through a lower-intensity (sublime and sublimated) love—which is to say, not in isolation from the ego, but in its giving way to something larger, which might also be smaller.

That's not a bad place to start when it comes to what one needs to know as a writer, or even as a reader or scholar or serious seeker, though of course one comes to such things only long after the start.

Then again, one is always starting.

ACKNOWLEDGMENTS

Grateful acknowledgment is due to the editors and publishers of the books in which these poems first appeared: *Rift*, Station Hill Press; *Hymns & Qualms*, Sheep Meadow Press; *Things on Which I've Stumbled* and *The Invention of Influence*, New Directions. Previously published translations appear here courtesy of Princeton University Press (*The Dream of the Poem: Hebrew Poetry from Muslim and Christian Spain, 950– 1492*, 2007; *Selected Poems of Solomon Ibn Gabirol*, 2001; and *Selected Poems of Shmuel HaNagid*, 1996); Yale University Press (*The Poetry of Kabbalah: Mystical Verse from the Jewish Tradition*, 2012); New Directions and Aharon Shabtai (*J'accuse*, 2003, and *War & Love, Love & War: Selected Poems*, 2010, by Aharon Shabtai); Ibis Editions and Harold Schimmel (*From Island to Island* by Harold Schimmel, 1998); Copper Canyon Press and the estate of Taha Muhammad Ali (*So What: New & Selected Poems* by Taha Muhammad Ali, 2006); Ibis Editions, the Institute for the Translation of Hebrew Literature, and the estate of Avraham Ben Yitzhak, Dvir Gallery, Tel Aviv (*Collected Poems of Avraham Ben Yitzhak*, 2003). Translations of poems by Leah Goldberg appear courtesy of HaKibbutz HaMeuchad, and of poems by Natan Zach courtesy of the author.

Earlier versions of these poems and translations were first published in the following journals: *AGNI*, *Aldeburgh Poetry Paper*, *Alligatorzine*, *Almost Island*, *American Letters & Commentary*, *The American Scholar*, *Circumference*, *Colorado Review*, *Common Knowledge*, *Conjunctions*, *Critical Quarterly*, *Delos*, *Financial Times*, *The Forward*, *Grand Street*, *Hambone*, *Der Hammer*, *Island*, *The Jerusalem Post*, *The Liberal*, *Lingo*, *London Review of Books*, *LVNG*, *The Lyric*, *Mandorla*, *Narrative*, *The Nation*, *No*, *Northern Lights*, *The Paris Review*, *Parnassus*, *Partisan Review*, *Pequod*, *Plume*, *Poetry*,

Poetry Nation, *The Poetry Review*, *Princeton Library Chronicle*, *Scripsi*, *Shearsman*, *Stonecutter*, *Sulfur*, *Talisman*, *The Times Literary Supplement*, *TriQuarterly*, *The Yale Review*, and *Zeek*.

*

For aid, abetment, and admonition in the making of this collection, echoing thanks are due to Mark Kamine, Eli Gottlieb, Gerald Stern, Gabriel Levin, Harold Schimmel, Robert Cohen, Aharon Shabtai, Eliot Weinberger, Stanley Moss, Barbara Epler, Annie Kantar, Jeanne Bloom, Harold Bloom, Christian Wiman, Langdon Hammer, Nathan Thrall, Judy Heiblum, Joshua Cohen, Michael Silverblatt, Jonathan Boyd, John Knight, and Joel Shapiro.

And finally, to Jonathan Galassi, for his faith in the shape and scope of this book, for his advice and his example—only hymns.

A Note About the Author

Peter Cole was born in Paterson, New Jersey, in 1957. The author of four previous books of poems and many volumes of translations from Hebrew and Arabic, he has received numerous honors for his work, including an American Academy of Arts and Letters Award in Literature, a Guggenheim Foundation Fellowship, a National Jewish Book Award, and a MacArthur Fellowship. He divides his time between Jerusalem and New Haven.